BFI Modern Classics

D1579095

orm
ubject

d
nema is

motion
e
of
n
of
it,
hat

L'Argent

Kent Jones

First published in 1999 by the
British Film Institute
21 Stephen Street, London W1P 2LN

Copyright © Kent Jones 1999

Reprinted 2009

The British Film Institute is the UK national
agency with responsibility for encouraging
the arts of film and television and conserving
them in the national interest.

Series design by Andrew Barron &
Collis Clements Associates

Typeset in Italian Garamond and Swiss 721BT
by D R Bungay Associates, Burghfield, Berks

Printed in Great Britain

British Library Cataloguing-in-Publication Data
A catalogue record for this book is available
from the British Library
ISBN 0-85170-733–5/978-0-85170-733-4

Contents

Acknowledgments

I have a number of people to thank: Bob Hunter, Jonathan Rosenbaum, Nicolas Saada and David Thompson for supplying me with videotapes; John Belton, Nicole Brenez, John Gianvito, Peter Gizzi, Benoit Jacquot, Phillip Lopate, Mark McElhatten, Adrian Martin, Dominique Paini, Jonathan Rosenbaum and Gavin Smith for creative discussions and all-around help; James Quandt, for putting up with me and offering very sensitive commentary on my initial writings about the film; my wife Maria and my sons Ethan and Andrezj, for their patience, support and love; my kind editor Rob White for his even greater patience; Michael Gizzi, for helping me to pay attention to the soundtracks in Bresson's films; and Olivier Assayas, a good friend, a mind as tough and sharp as they come and a great film-maker, who more than anyone else helped me to think about *L'Argent*.

This book is dedicated to Frank Moore.

On Bresson

How do you deal with a film-maker as profoundly individualistic and idiosyncratic as Robert Bresson? Every aspect of Bresson's cinema – visualization of space, storytelling practice, sound, performance style – is so much the product of his unique temperament and vision that his work has prompted extreme reactions from every quarter. For many average cinemagoers, his films feel disturbingly unemotional. In a parallel with popular reactions to atonal music and abstract painting, the lack of emotional variance in Bresson's (non-) actors is felt as sharply as the lack of melody in Webern or the lack of representation in Mondrian: in each case, the charge is excessive intellectual and formal precision at the expense of emotional involvement, hence anti-populism and élitism. On the other hand, for those cinemagoers who do connect with his work, Bresson is all but infallible. And for those who take it upon themselves to explain this towering artist, he remains a bit of a puzzle.

First, there is the approach of unbounded awe, in which Bresson's films are deemed to be so inhumanly pure that they stand far outside the rest of cinema, inhabiting a rarefied atmosphere uniquely their own. This line of thinking is perhaps best represented by the Bresson entry in David Thomson's *Biographical Dictionary of Film*, in which he writes:

It might be said that to watch Bresson is to risk conversion away from the cinema. His meaning is so clearly inspirational, and his treatment so remorselesoly interior, that he seems to shame the extrinsic glamour and extravagance of movies. For that reason alone, he is not an easy director to digest. To go beyond admiration might be too near surrender.[1]

The flip side is represented by Pauline Kael in her various writings on Bresson throughout the years. According to Kael, Bresson began his career doing great work but, beginning with *Pickpocket* (1959), slid steadily into the mire of formal and thematic severity. In other words, his films may be great on some level, but they are far too punishing to actually enjoy; therefore, they deserve banishment from the populist kingdom of the

Robert Bresson shooting *Trial of Joan of Arc*

movies. Both points of view are governed by the commonly-held idea of the average cinemagoer who needs a little sugar to make the harsh medicine of truth go down easily. Moreover, these points of view are founded in the oft-repeated characterization of Bresson's cinema as 'austere', 'severe' and 'ascetic', words used by his admirers as often as his detractors.

Second, there is Bresson the transcendental artist. This line of thought originates with Paul Schrader's *Transcendental Style in Film*, which concentrates only on Bresson's 'prison quartet' – *Diary of a Country Priest* (1950), *A Man Escaped* (1956), *Pickpocket* and *Trial of Joan of Arc* (1962). Schrader recognizes in those films a set of aesthetic properties that qualify them for membership in a cross-cultural artistic 'tradition', which posits reality as nothing more than a veil over the divine, or the infinite. Schrader's book has prompted a contrary position, articulated by Jonathan Rosenbaum, asserting that Bresson is not a religious artist at all, but in fact the ultimate materialist. This quarrel strikes me as peculiarly American, boiling down to a debate over whether existence itself should be viewed through a spiritual (i.e. Christian) or political (i.e. Marxist, or at the very least anti-capitalist) lens.

Third is the formalist Bresson – his film-making is so precise that it lends itself easily to formalist conceptions of cinema. His œuvre has been the site of numerous formal inquiries, the most excellent and persuasive of which have been collected by James Quandt in the critical volume he edited to accompany the touring package of Bresson's films that he recently curated out of the Ontario Cinémathèque. The bulk of the explicitly formalist writings on Bresson revolve around the concept of absence, of a cinema designed to evoke the unsayable and the unknowable. Such a position dovetails rather neatly with Schrader's position, although without his spiritual trappings.

In what I take to be the best writing on Bresson – by André Bazin, René Prédal and Raymond Durgnat – the posture is less one of awe than admiration, and the films are dealt with as individual cases. In his essay written specifically for Quandt's book, Durgnat takes a fascinating (and quite typical, for anyone familiar with his criticism) scattershot approach to Bresson's work, throwing out myriad ways of classifying this supposedly

Pickpocket; the like-minded Paul Schrader ending of *American Gigolo*

unclassifiable film-maker. If there is one common thread that runs through all the writing on Bresson, it is the overall impression of an immense, severe and very exacting artist, whose rigour is so complete that it borders on the systematic, serving as a sort of conduit to aspects of existence that are beyond words, hence beyond identification, but which can none the less be felt.

In fact, we might say this about all the artists who we admire. But in Bresson's case, his human touch, the discussion of which is at the heart of popular criticism, is absent. The portrait of this particular artist, aided and abetted by the oracular pronouncements on cinema in his own book and the few interviews he's given, is generally tinged with mysticism. Bresson comes off as a rather daunting figure with a purchase on ultimate reality, a divinely gifted spiritual authority. He is the Blaise Pascal of cinema, who works within but is not of it, and hence whose relationship to his own material is impersonal, his choices apparently systematic. There is the strong sense of a terminally introspective figure with little interest in the world around him, since his gaze is so inwardly directed. Even in the most earthbound writing on Bresson, there remains a tone of shivering veneration. If criticism is, among other things, a form of portraiture, then the collected writings on Bresson paint a portrait not of a human being, but of a super-human enigma. When considered altogether, the many different, equally emphatic forms of inquiry into his films become a kind of rough equivalent to Bresson's own manner of depicting space in sharply defined fragments, with Bresson himself at the unknowable centre.

How is it that Bresson has come to be regarded as more than just another great artist? How is it that his films supposedly exist outside of the normal currents of cinema, and that every one is seen as a meta-cinematic experience? Has there ever been another film-maker whose formal choices have been so exhaustively analysed, often with the hope that at the end of the line a purely figural 'counter-cinema' will be revealed, untainted by all the dreaded vices – identification, amplification (through music, camera movement, editing frenzy, theatrical performance style), representation. As Bresson himself has all but stated in his book, like an early Christian looking for converts, his is the true cinema, unpolluted by the vagaries of fashion. Like many great artists, Tolstoy in particular, Bresson has his overbearing and pompous side. If we were to take his *Notes on the Cinematographer* at face value, we would all believe that he alone has unlocked and opened the door to pure artistic expression in the cinema. In his view, anyone who works with a pre-established star has instantly forfeited his or her artistic integrity. Bresson's own description of his dissatisfaction with the actresses in *Les Anges du péché* (1943), his first feature, is not unlike the youth in *The Devil, Probably* (1977) who walks into church and feels the presence of God vanish the moment the priest arrives. However, his own counsel aside, no one has ever given up on the rest of cinema after seeing a Bresson film, at least no one that I've ever known. But somehow, the illusion that such a thing might occur persists.

'The demand for order', wrote Meyer Schapiro in his 1960 essay 'On the Humanity of Abstract Painting',

through which the new is condemned, is a demand for a certain kind of order, in disregard of the infinity of orders that painters have created and will continue to create. I do not refer here to the desire for a new order, but rather to the requirement of an already known order, familiar and reassuring.[2]

Such a demand, for an 'already known' order, colours a great deal of the thinking on Bresson by both his admirers and his detractors. It's not uncommon to posit artists as extraordinary as Bresson beyond the historical continuum of their art form, since the novelty of their work demands that the very terms on which we all agree suddenly be made to shift like sub-continental tectonic plates. Far simpler to take them on their own terms and see their work as a radical break that nullifies everything before it. Given the extremity of the situation, it's far better to do as Durgnat and Prédal have done and cast their critical nets wide. 'The problem of abstract art', as Schapiro writes, 'like that of all new styles, is a problem of practical criticism and not of theory ... ' In the simplest possible terms, the question becomes: how do we make a human being out of Robert Bresson, and respect his greatness at the same time?

There is a similar problem with that other great figure of modern cinema, John Cassavetes, who is in many ways Bresson's opposite. In both cases there is a critical tendency to be overwhelmed, and hence to fixate on a single trait (Bresson's formal rigour, Cassavetes' behavioural extravagance). In both cases, we are dealing with artists who reject most of the norms in their chosen art form, and consequently regard their own working methods as the only truthful ones; both are thought by their admirers to inhabit a sphere of purity far beyond the commercially tainted realm of cinema; and both are extraordinary artists who have accomplished what Griffith and Welles did before them, something that neither criticism nor normal viewing habits are well-equipped to digest, and that film theory, with its extremely alienated position in regard to film production and its atomized, a-critical approach to the medium, is unable to describe. And that is to push cinema, through the force of their own genius, up to a new level, expanding on hitherto latent possibilities and realigning the parameters of the film experience to their own ends. They are not unlike inventors forced to fabricate entirely new objects in order to construct the larger object that exists only in their mind's eye.

Many people who love Bresson's work have no love for Cassavetes' and vice versa. And it seems certain that, in the event that either of them ever had the opportunity to see the other's work, they would have been repulsed. But as Schapiro counsels, the real lesson lies in the fact that Bresson and Cassavetes exist simultaneously, poles apart in every way imaginable, within the same world – that of cinema. No doubt many of us love both of them, but how often have we ever considered the bracing, salutory fact of two such diametrically opposed world-views existing side by side?

What is it that makes Bresson's art feel so eternally new and disorienting? To my eyes, it's not transcendence (Schrader), nor is it the displacement of the metaphorical by the figural (Sitney), nor is it Jansenism. 'Some of the most important things movies can do are in this film,' Manny Farber once wrote of *Mouchette* (1966), in a tone far less reverent and distanced than most of the writing on Bresson. Earlier in the piece, he describes Nadine Nordier's incarnation of Mouchette.

Nadine Nordier's 'somber dignity' in *Mouchette*

Nordier's singularity is tied to painful effects: apathetic about her well-being, hair uncombed and probably lice-ridden, a large part of the painfulness has to do with large lumpy legs, stockings that won't stay up, big shoes. Despite all these humiliations, she is never cartoony and gets enormous somber dignity into her walking tours, combats with other girls, and a terrific moment when she climbs into bed, wet from a rainstorm, and then goes into some slovenly chores for the baby.[3]

Bresson is not often thought of in such terms – as a portraitist. More often than not, his films are defined according to their formal and thematic choices, as opposed to the actual onscreen material. We don't often think of Bresson in terms of his rendering of reality, of lived experience. He's usually pitted against everyone else, and singled out for his unorthodox way of depicting action through a complex set of formal relations that require disassembly and examination.

Yet listen to Bresson speaking to Michel Ciment for a 1983 *Positif* interview:

You have to go with your sensibility. There is nothing else. I've been called an intellectual, but of course I'm not. Writing is unbelievably difficult, but I have to do it, because everything must originate with me. I've been called a Jansenist, which is madness. I'm the opposite. I'm interested in impressions. I'll give you an example, taken from *L'Argent*. When I'm on the Grands Boulevards, the first thing I think is *How do they impress me?* And the answer is that they impress me as a mass of legs and a sound of feet on the pavements. I tried to communicate this impression by picture and by sound … There has to be a shock at the moment of doing, there has to be a feeling that the humans and things to be filmed are new, you have to throw surprises on film. That's what happened in the scene on the Grands Boulevards … I could feel the steps, I focused on the protagonist's legs, and that way I could propel him through the crowd to where he needed to be. That's the Grands Boulevards, as far as I'm concerned, all the motion. Otherwise, I might as well have used a picture postcard. The thing that struck me when I used to go to the cinema was that everything had been *wanted* in advance, down to the last detail … Painters do not know in advance how their picture is going to turn out, a sculptor cannot tell what his sculpture will be, a poet does not plan a poem in advance …

You will have noticed that in *L'Argent* there are a series of close-ups whose only function is to add sensation. When the father, a piano-player, drops a glass, his daughter is in the kitchen. Her dustpan and sponge are ready. I do not then enter the room, but cut immediately to a close shot which I like very much, the wet floor with the sound of the sponge. That is music, rhythm, sensation … Increasingly, what I am after – and with *L'Argent* it became almost a working method – is to communicate the impressions I feel.[4]

I think that this need to give form to his own impressions, more than any system, sense of transcendence, or degree of 'moral accountability', as Tony Pipolo has so aptly phrased it,[5] is at the core of Bresson's art and its unusual impact. The type of 'sensation' that Bresson is describing is felt only fitfully in the work of most other film-makers. The many shots from

The glass perched on the piano, about to 'add sensation'

the inside of moving cars in Nicholas Ray's *On Dangerous Ground* (1951), for instance, or the episode with the broken-down boxer arriving at his hotel room in John Huston's *Fat City* (1972), are powerful sensory experiences, in which the film-makers have clearly sought and achieved a human (i.e. personal, subjective) sense of duration, space, rhythm, the texture of reality as they perceive it. However, these are isolated instances in films that, like most other works, leave behind the purely sensory to make way for the rhetorical, the poetic, the point of view of the protagonist or the purely functional. Farber's comments about Huston's *The Asphalt Jungle* (1950) could apply just as well to a Bresson film: 'Two exquisite cinematic moments: the safe-cracker, one hand already engaged, removing the cork from the nitro bottle with his teeth; the sharp, clean thrust of the chisel as it slices through the wooden strut.'[6] The very feel of the world, in which there is no hierarchy of attention and even the most apparently meaningless event has its own integrity and its own special thrill, has been central to Farber since his beginnings as a critic – he is not indulging in idle appreciation here. It's also central to Bresson, and it informs every moment of his cinema (it's worth noting here that Bresson began as a painter, and that Farber remains one). The sense of reality existing only through the filter of personal perception becomes more and more central to Bresson as time goes on, and it accounts for many of the more idiosyncratic aspects of his work: the unique syntax that has been developing since *Les Anges du péché* and that owes almost nothing to the presentational; an evolution from spiritual self-recognition in individuals, in narratives that seem exemplary and almost out of time, towards an increasingly disenchanted accounting of the hindrances that young people encounter on the road to that self-recognition, in narratives increasingly connected to their contemporary moment; the feeling that every character in Bresson's work remains a stranger, that the intimacy of his films remains the intimacy of an observer rather than an empathetic identifying participant; the pull toward moments that 'add sensation', as Bresson himself put it, such as the organist cleaning his instrument as a prelude to the church meeting in *The Devil, Probably*, or the close-up of the oil pump pulled from the pipe and snaked back onto the truck in *L'Argent*.

It may be true that Bresson's films feel like pristine, ascetic objects in relation to the rest of cinema, but I think that's purely a function of his painterly search for a completely personal imprint of experience, so that every moment of every film is not just philosophically but *gesturally* his own, just as every brushstroke of Cézanne's is markedly *his* own. Bresson has often said that he gave up his painter's eye when he started to make films, but he never gave up his painter's sensibility: he understood that the total work was not the frame but the film itself, in which each shot, each gesture, is like a brushstroke. Every sequence in Bresson's cinema, from the flurry of hands slipping in and out of pockets and pocketbooks in the *Pickpocket* free-for-all to the car hitting the oil slick in *Au Hasard, Balthazar* (1966), from the continual, brutal returns to Dominique Sanda's body in her coffin in *Une Femme douce* (1969) to the disruptive vacuum cleaner going over the rug in *The Devil, Probably*, is what we would call 'privileged'. There is nothing illustrative, nothing purely mechanical, nothing intentionally more spellbinding than anything else, either on the rhythmic, hyper-attentive soundtrack or in the 'flattened' (Bresson's own word) image, always shot with a 50-millimeter lens. What happens is that those flattened images and always-specific sounds meet to create what Bresson has rightly called a three-dimensional effect. Thus, the concentration on the scraping of bits of a broken wine glass over a polished wooden floor with a wet sponge gives the floor, the glass, the wine, the sunlight through the window, the hollowness of the room, and the immediacy of the situation (the glass has broken because it's been carelessly perched on the edge of a piano by a drunken old patriarch; his daughter has heard the crash and automatically gone to fetch a sponge to clean up the mess) a *presence*, a reverberation. It's a thrilling example of Bresson's approach: each scene charted out almost ploddingly, like a mapmaker charting a landscape; step by step, vigorously taken, through the narrative; a supersensitive care with what gesture will impart the most narrative information but also convey the greatest wealth of experience; a staccato accent on almost everything (you get the feeling that for Bresson, lingering on a scene is the equivalent of a musician giving a virtuoso performance, thus detracting from the beauty of the music itself). It's the strange mixture of careful planning with the spontaneous shock of perception that gives Bresson's cinema its special brand of vertiginousness.

One could easily say that the uniformity of Bresson's cinema from *A Man Escaped* on, the fact that every moment is equally alive, results from his belief in a Christian universe, where there is no room for the kinds of ego-centred upsets, questions and disturbances that are at the centre of Cassavetes' work, over in the far corner of cinema. As written above, characters remain strangers in Bresson's films, and our contact with them is never complicitous in the way it is in 99 per cent of the rest of cinema. But isn't that simply because he's giving us a God's-eye view of the world?

'Actually, every doctrinal hint I thought I found seemed, in the end, to lead away from intellectual exactness – while remaining firmly within a *sacred* sphere,' Raymond Durgnat has written of Bresson.[7] As 'perfect' as his films seem, as systematic and as governed by firm beliefs, there is no intellectual or spiritual last stop with Bresson's art – there is no key, either formal or religious, that will unlock the door to ultimate meaning. I believe that what we are really experiencing with Bresson, on the most profound level, is something utterly singular in cinema: an intimate record of contact with the world, recreated and transmuted into narrative. For Bresson one of the most crucial components in the rendering of experience is the inflexible course of time, which can only be fully rendered (rather than evoked, or alluded to) by narrative. You might go so far as to say that Bresson makes films about the world first, and the things that happen within it second (it's not surprising that one of his long-cherished projects was a film based on Genesis), which is the reverse of what happens with most other film-makers. In most films, we get a sense of the world as it revolves around particular characters, feelings, situations, conflicts, states of being. In any given work by a particular film-maker, the world feels like a slightly different place. To take the example of Welles the world is forbiddingly monumental in *Citizen Kane* (1941), disappointing and prone to betrayal by time's passing in *The Magnificent Ambersons* (1942), a nightmarish comfort zone for malignance in *Touch of Evil* (1958). But only in Bresson does the world itself, in all its materiality, have an identity as fixed as the people who live within it. In Bresson, the world is vast, calm, surprising, unknowable yet seeable, touchable, hearable, unresponsive to individual desires and problems, and somehow miraculous.

Bresson's singular relationship with the material world is not at the centre of his art in the way it is for a process-oriented artist like Rivette or Michael Snow. He is and always has been a classical storyteller and a moralist as well, albeit a moralist of a very particular type: his films are never prescriptive or cautionary, but rather, as Thomson has put it so well, demonstrative. However, I think that it's Bresson's intimate record of his own contact with the world that is at the centre of our *fascination* with his films, and of the extraordinary beauty it holds for those of us with eyes to see it. Because film had always been sold as *the* popular, inherently democratic art form, the idea of film spectatorship has remained quite rigid, certainly far more rigid than the idea of the spectator of opera or painting or dance. The idea that films are mandated to provide identification, involvement, catharsis, through a set of conventions that we all supposedly recognize and share, may seem frivolous and arbitrary to those of us who appreciate Straub–Godard–Oliveira. But the idea remains a powerful one that shouldn't be underestimated, and it's given rise to a number of divisive, exclusionary terms – 'festival film', 'art-house hermeticism', and even the term 'foreign film'. And that's why it's so important to insist on the fact that Bresson is not *rejecting* anything, but rather *embracing* his own set of rules. He is imagining a viewer who is able to watch his films with the same patience and spirit of adventure that we automatically associate with spectatorship in the other arts. And he is asking that viewer to see his film as a whole rather than to be driven along or swept away by it, the same way that we would step back and examine the entire composition of a Matisse or a Cézanne.

If you look at Bresson's films in succession, you can see his power to render his own impressions becoming more and more acute. The effect on younger film-makers, particularly film-makers who grew up during the final phase of his career, is incalculable. I once had a conversation with Claire Denis about her film *S'en Fout la mort* (1990), in which she told me that she had been spellbound (and influenced) simply by the way that Bresson showed the exchange of money in both *Pickpocket* and *L'Argent*.

Trust (Hal Hartley, 1990); *I Hired a Contract Killer* (Aki Kaurismaki, 1990)

Olivier Assayas once spoke of the way he and his teenage friends cracked jokes at a screening of *The Devil, Probably* when it came out in 1977, followed by his realization when he saw the film again many years later that Bresson had captured his generation, and the way they related to the world around them, with startling exactitude. In both cases, it's the beauty with which Bresson rendered objects and sensations, in a world that they recognized not as some spiritual construct, but as the one they lived in. And one can clearly feel the *physical* influence of Bresson in the work of film-makers from all over the world, from Darezhan Omirbaev in

Killer; Une Nouvelle vie

Kazakhstan (particularly in his most recent film, *Killer*) to Aki Kaurismaki in Finland. In Assayas' *Une Nouvelle vie* (1993), it's in the way that the director builds his film around the strange textures and sonorities of the digital world. In the films of Hal Hartley, it's felt less in the deliberately toneless vocal delivery of his actors than in the careful segmenting and partitioning of space. And of course, in each case, the final result is vastly different. Which is as it should be. Because the lesson that Bresson's work teaches anyone who is attentive to it is that when you make a film, you must resist all conventions and stick to the world as you and only you experience it. He and no one else has made the intensity of perception a central component of the cinematic experience.

On *The Forged Coupon*

L'Argent is adapted from *The Forged Coupon*, also known as *The False Coupon* or *The Forged Banknote*, which was finished by Tolstoy in 1904, three years after his excommunication from the Russian Orthodox Church. Tolstoy's belief in a true Christianity shorn of politics and vulgar ceremony put him in bitter conflict with both the Church and the Tsar from the early 1880s up to his death.

After a spiritual crisis in the late 1870s, Tolstoy renounced the materialistic trappings of his life and repudiated the works that had made him a legendary figure. He dedicated his life to providing aid and shelter to the poor, and counselled his rich friends to do the same. Although he was no Marxist, he preached (through his writings and public pronouncements) the upheaval of all contemporary forms of government

The former Count Leo Tolstoy in his later years

and organized religion in order to make way for a truly equitable way of life. Although possession of Tolstoy's writings could result in severe punishment, his work was widely circulated in foreign editions, manuscripts and hectographed copies (copies struck from gelatin plates). His influence was somewhat deflated and lessened by the failed revolution of 1905, after which his espousal of non-violent resistance (later to be used to advantage by Gandhi, who had begun a lengthy correspondence with Tolstoy at the beginning of the century) was called archaic and beside the point. Neverthless, when Tolstoy died in 1910, Maxim Gorki declared that the world had come to a halt.

Tolstoy essentially saw the teachings of the Church as a distortion of Christian truth, in which the Church, and by extension the government, had usurped the role of repository of truth and faith from God. This was the kernel of his message in his polemical writings, such as 'What Is Art?' or 'A Confession', the 1879 work that marks the beginning of his metamorphosis from mere author to moral guide. And it was also at the centre of his fiction during this last period, when he endeavoured to write simple tales that could be understood by peasants. *The Forged Coupon* was Tolstoy's last novella, widely read during his life but only officially published one year after his death. Not to slight him with historical hindsight, but its flowing vision of life represents a viewpoint that could only exist for a member of the landed gentry and self-ordained representative of the downtrodden, with its elevated, distanced view of the Russian people.

The narrative, which takes place over the course of roughly fifteen years and in a variety of city and country locations, is dispersed among twenty-four separate characters – one of whom is Tolstoy's nemesis Tsar Nicholas – many of whom cross paths with one another only briefly, or never at all. The action moves along by relay, with an artful simplicity. The first half traces a line downward to the depths of degradation, while the second half tilts upward to the light of redemption. Certain characters are merely functional, some are given thumbnail sketches as contemporary types with whom Tolstoy clearly has a beef (he reserves the most scorn and devotes the most negative detailing to a pompous religious instructor and rising church star). Many of the most admirable characters are treated to hardly any detail at all, as though their goodness was so pure that it was simply *there,* and thus required no description. The bulk of the story is taken up by two characters, one of whom murders the other during their one and only encounter.

Tolstoy and Bresson begin at the same point. Fedor Mikhailovich refuses his adolescent son Mitya an advance on his allowance. Mitya pleads with his mother for the loan, and she promises to help him but is unable to do anything until the banks open the next morning. Mitya's friend Makhin solves the problem by taking Mitya's coupon (a pre-revolutionary equivalent to currency, clipped from an interest-bearing document) and changing the amount with his pen. The two boys go to a photography store and use it to buy a cheap picture frame. The proprietress, Mar'ya Vasil'evna, is subsequently bawled out by her husband Evgeny Mikhailovich, who later passes the forged note on to a poor peasant selling loose bundles of firewood.

The peasant, named Ivan Mironov, tries to use the forged note at a local tavern, and when the bartender insists on holding on to it as evidence, Mironov flies into a rage, and he is arrested. The next morning, he leads the cops to Evgeny Mikhailovich's house. When he is questioned, Mikhailovich denies meeting Mironov or receiving goods from him, and so does his groundskeeper Vasily, to whom Mikhailovich has slipped five rubles – he gets ten more rubles to lie in court. The judge finds in favour of Mikhailovich, who magnanimously offers to pay the court costs. Vasily resolves to become as immoral and mercenary as the wealthy city-dwellers who employ him. Mikhailovich eventually catches him stealing, and dismisses him without pressing charges.

Bresson drops the next part of the story, which takes place on the farm of a grandiose liberal named Petr Nikolaevich. When he finds that his horses have been stolen, he develops an intense hatred of peasants in general and directs the bulk of his fury at a lazy, arrogant (though innocent) man named Proshka. The real horse thief is none other than Ivan Mironov, a former disgruntled employee of Nikolaevich.

Bresson picks up the story again as Tolstoy returns to Evgeny Mikhailovich and Mar'ya Vasil'evna, who is unable to forgive herself for being duped by those two students. One day, she sees Makhin walking down the street, but he contorts his features into such an ugly face that she doesn't recognize him. However, she does recognize Mitya, and has a word with his religion instuctor, Mikhail Vvedensky. Vvedensky, who has enough spiritual pride for an army of believers, is still smarting from a run-in the year before with Mitya's father (over his 'dismally liberal', anti-clerical views), and he takes it upon himself to publicly shame Mitya, who promptly confesses to his mother. The mother visits the photography shop, pays off Mar'ya Vasil'evna and persuades her not to give Mitya's name to the police – she also warns Mitya to deny everything when he is confronted by his father.

'Meanwhile' – the word comes up frequently in this story – Vasily takes a long, reinvigorating job as the night watchman of a farm. When the season is over, he goes back to Moscow, breaks into Evgeny Mikhailovich's shop and cleans out all the cash on the premises (sharply visualized in the film). Ivan Mironov is caught red-handed by the peasant owners of some of the horses he's stolen and beaten to death. A hulking man named Stepan Pelageyushkin is charged with the murder, and sentenced to a year in jail, during which his family is reduced to begging in the streets, his wife dies and his home is seized by creditors (Bresson combines this episode with many of the details of Stepan's next and last stay in prison). The day he is released from prison, he goes to an inn, murders the owner and his mistress with their own axe (a detail Bresson places later in the story), steals their money and leaves.

Tolstoy introduces Mariya Semenovna, an older woman of infinite goodness, patience and simplicity – she is the basis for the unnamed woman played by Sylvie van den Elsen, one of the greatest characters in Bresson's œuvre. She lives with and cares for her father, sister, brother-in-law and nephew, most of them drunks, all of whom beat her. During a visit to town from her house in the country, she meets a tailor, on whom she leaves a mighty and permanent impression with her essential goodness.

Bresson drops the next, large portion of the story. In a direct contrast to this happy encounter, Tolstoy 'cuts' back to Petr Nikolaevich, who has rented out his own land and taken a job as the head of a nearby estate – at every available opportunity, he punishes the local peasants. During a showdown over grazing rights, for which he demands money, he accidentally shoots a peasant and is beaten to death and dumped into a ravine. Two men are charged with the murder and sentenced to death.

Tolstoy returns to the tailor, who, thanks to the influence of Mariya Semenovna, has taken his first step on the path of a righteous Christian life. He starts bible study classes in his house, and acquires a follower named Ivan Chuev. A true Christian movement begins to form, and when word reaches the church, Vvedensky, now known as Father Misail, is sent to intervene. He delivers a sermon to the regular churchgoers about the dangers of sectarianism, and in response they form a mob and attack the dissidents. Ivan Chuev puts out the eye of one of his attackers in self-defense and is sentenced to exile. As a result of his intercession, Father Misail is made an archimandrite.

Tolstoy then goes back two years to a political firebrand named Katya Turchaninova. She and her fellow student Tyurin spend the summer on his family's estate, located next to the estate managed by Petr Nikolaevich, where the two young revolutionaries try to educate the peasants. During the trial of Nikolaevich's murderers, Tyurin is implicated and arrested. Katya Turchaninova makes endless entreaties to various officials in an attempt to free Tyurin, and finally she buys a gun and shows up at the office of the regional minister. She lets him flirt with her before she fires her weapon and misses him at point blank range. An investigation is conducted into the 'conspiracy', and she is imprisoned.

Bresson picks up the story with the return to Mariya Semenovna, who, as she is collecting her pension money, bumps into a stranger: we know that it's Stepan, who in the meantime has also murdered a woman and her children. When Mariya Semenovna gets back to her house, she notices that he has been following her. That night, Stepan sneaks in and murders everyone in sight before he gets to Mariya Semenovna. 'Where's the money?' he asks, and she challenges him: 'Why are you doing this? Is it really necessary?' She reminds him that he is destroying souls the moment before he slits her throat. Stepan finds the money, and that's the end of his murder spree. Haunted by Mariya Semenovna's face and words, he spends a sleepless day and night before he walks into a bar and confesses to a policeman. In prison, he tries to hang himself, but the rope breaks (Bresson places the suicide attempt earlier, during the film's equivalent to Stepan's first stay in prison) – and here Bresson drops out again. In a dream, Stepan asks Mariya Semenovna to forgive him, and he is finally able to live with himself. He is put in a cell block with Ivan Chuev and Vasily, where he listens intently to Chuev's readings from Matthew. Gradually, he becomes a respected figure, and a feared one as well. When he's placed in solitary for picking a fight, he learns to read his favourite passages in the bible with the help of a guard. And when he leaves solitary, he starts a bible study group with Vasily and another prisoner named Makhorkin, an executioner. Under Stepan's influence, Makhorkin refuses to execute the two men who have been convicted of killing Petr Nikolaevich.

Makhin, the high school forgerer, is now a court investigator. He questions Stepan, and he too is profoundly affected by his moral and spiritual certainty. He relates the whole story of Stepan to his wealthy fiancée Liza Eropkina, and she is so moved that she makes up her mind to give away all the land in her name (an autobiographical detail for the author). Vasily asks Stepan to help him escape, and once he makes it out he's sheltered by the girl who had run to tell Petr Nikolaevich's wife, Natal'ya Ivanovna, that he had been murdered. Tolstoy shifts to the widow, one of the most finely drawn characters in the story. After an initial surge of liberation on hearing the news of her dreaded husband's murder, she compensates with a lust for vengeance. On the scheduled day of the execution, she hides in her house. When she's later told that the executioner has refused to do his duty, she suddenly begs for them to be pardoned, and has the local constabulary officer help her write a letter to the Tsar.

Now Tolstoy starts moving with breathtaking speed from character to character. Liza Eropkina's father sends her to a learned monk named Isidor in the hope that he'll talk her out of her foolhardy plan, but *she* winds up winning *him* over. Because of her influence, Isidor becomes a renowned preacher. Vasily, in the meantime, has become a renowned

Robin Hood figure. When he's captured and sentenced to exile, he accepts his fate cheerfully. The Tsar receives Natal'ya Ivanovna's letter but refuses to pardon the two peasants, and eventually someone is found to execute them. Isidor has achieved such renown that he's called to preach before the Tsar, and in his sermon he questions the use of capital punishment in a Christian country. He is promptly seized and detained, then sent to the Suzdal monastery, presided over by none other than ... good old Father Misail. Tolstoy briefly returns to his old enemy the Tsar, to recount the effect of Isidor's words on his conscience. In a beautiful passage, he writes that 'it was only from a distance that he saw the human being in himself.'[8]

Back to prison, where Proshka has ended up, sick from tuberculosis after a debauched life. He is placed in the infirmary, where he's comforted by Stepan. He reassures Proshka that there is redemption, offering himself as an example, and helps him to achieve a peaceful passage to the beyond.

In a little episode that Bresson drops into the middle of the film, and the last bit of Tolstoy's story of which he makes use, we return to Evgeny Mikhailovich, who is about to lose his business. Just when he and his wife are complaining about Vasily and exclaiming how easily he had lied to the police, an envelope arrives with four hundred ruble notes and a letter from their former employee, making amends to both them and Ivan Mironov. As he reads the letter, tears well up in Evgeny Mikhailovich's eyes.

Isidor is held in the Suzdal prison with thirteen other clergymen. When he is visited by Misail, he exclaims: 'Brother! What are you doing? You have broken with all that is holy!' Father Misail orders his release, along with seven of the other penitents, and quietly retires to a monastery.

Ten years later, we begin where we started, with Mitya. He is now a gold mining engineer in Siberia, and when he is sent to travel throughout the region on business it is suggested that he take Stepan – who is now regarded as a true holy man – with him. He is so affected by Stepan, who cares for everyone who crosses his path, that he gives up drinking and gambling, and turns down a lucrative position in order to lead a stable, helpful life. He reconciles with his father, Fedor Mikhailovich, who has long since abandoned his family. Scornful at first, the father suddenly remembers 'how many times he had been guilty before his son'.

Bresson has said that his admiration for Tolstoy's story 'about how evil spreads' did not prevent him from removing all references to Christianity and the Gospels, since his aim was to treat a modern form of indifference that is essentially unconscious. Which raises the question: why this particular story, which he strips for parts and refashions into an object so completely different from its source as to be almost unrecognizable as an adaptation? In all of his previous literary adaptations, Bresson essentially respects the form of his original material, even when he has turned its intentions inside out. In *Four Nights of a Dreamer* (1971), for instance, adapted from Dostoevsky's *White Nights*, Bresson throws out the morbidly romantic fantasizing of Dostoevsky's hero, a young functionary, and replaces it with the gentler but (in Bresson's eyes) more insidious self-consciousness of the post-May '68 generation. But even though Bresson embellishes a great deal on Dostoevsky's original and reorders its

Guillaume des Forêts and Isabelle Weingarten in *Four Nights of a Dreamer*

priorities, he sticks fairly close to its letter, as he does in his two Bernanos adaptations and his previous Dostoevsky adaptation, *Une Femme douce* (which sticks closer to the original – more than any other Bresson film, it's a psychological suspense story). *L'Argent* is something else again.

Unsurprisingly to anyone who has even a passing acquaintance with Bresson's cinema, he all but eliminates Tolstoy's editorializing. Tolstoy zeroes in on each character's individual version of usury in the first half of his story: Fedor Mikhailovich's duplicity with Ivan Mironov, Mironov's hawking of over-priced firewood, Vasily's initially cynical justification for stealing, Petr Nikolaevich's penny-pinching vision of the world. The author has an even greater horror of spiritual pride. Mikael Vvedensky/ Father Misail is endlessly chastised by his creator, and the political firebrand Katya Turchaninova is more gently upbraided – in fact, the warped spirits of these two find their way into the film through a character completely invented by Bresson, a cellmate of Yvon who gives him an obtuse lecture on the evil of money. Articulate loudmouths are recurring figures in late Bresson – the hiker in *Au Hasard, Balthazar*, the former classmate who stops by Jacques' apartment in *Four Nights of a Dreamer* (both characters give boorish art history lectures), the psychiatrist in *The Devil, Probably*. In each instance, one can feel Bresson's bristling displeasure with pontification in general, and the stark contrast between these moments and the rest of the film around them – a sudden, indiscriminate gush of vain words amidst a flow of action – betrays a fascinating tic, as though Bresson himself had suffered many such fools disturbing his concentration in everyday life.

The second half of the story is rife with biblical passages and quotations, most notably the two long sections from Matthew that mark the beginning of Stepan's Christian education. They are offered as a stark contrast to the slovenly habits and self-regarding airs of the clergy. Since the action of *The Forged Coupon* spans so much time and incorporates so many characters, individual details and judgements pack a swift, vivid punch: Mar'ya Vasil'evna's 'laced, fingerless gloves', Petr Nikolaevich's ominous dark glasses, the 'darkness and narrowness of the phony environment' in which Liza Eropkina has grown up, and the decadence of the bishop who orders Father Misail to confront the rogue Christians. 'Try hard. I have suffered a great deal over my flock,' the bishop replied, leisurely extending his plump, white hand to take the cup of tea which the servant had just brought him. 'Is that all the jam? Bring some more.'

As greatly as Bresson professes to admire Tolstoy's story, I'm certain that he also found its transparent preachiness and philosophizing a bit difficult to take. Although Tolstoy fills the story with an impressive range of characters and behaviours, some of whom are as vividly drawn as anyone in his best work, the pattern in which they fit together has a disconcerting uniformity. Peasants are all misled creatures driven to devious means of eking out a living. The bourgeoisie – and by extension the clergy – is arrogant, self-satisfied, and takes considerable license in its treatment of those unfortunates stuck on the lowest rung of the economic ladder. The nation's leaders live at an unnatural distance from their own humanity, allowing them to view the world with deadening detachment. However, all of God's creatures, even the Tsar, are subject to influence. The chain of usury can be broken by a single, swift blow from the hammer of faith: once you step into the light, there is nothing but joy, and there is no turning back.

Tolstoy's psychological insight is frequently breathtaking (the imagination of Natal'ya Ivanovna's reaction formation is especially beautiful), but there's a wilfulness to his human tapestry, as though he had thrown a true-Christian net over all of (Russian) humanity. By this last phase of his life, polemics had overshadowed artistry. The vast scope of this story is supposedly from the omniscient (and hence transparent) point of view of God, but it is actually from the point of view of a world-renowned writer cum-spiritual leader, outdoing his rival the Tsar in munificence and offering a blueprint for Utopia in the form of a didactic tale that's free to circulate among the general population.

Such programmatic thinking, even on such a vast scale, is anathema to Bresson, who has always trusted in the potential of individual objects and sensations to reveal the grandeur of the world that contains them, without imposing a pattern of enlightenment over the behaviour of individuals. In Bresson's work, spiritual recognition feels like a profound form of self-recognition, far from the subtle fanaticism that overtakes characters in late Tolstoy, and it's never marked as the beginning of something permanent. It is also heavily dependent on chance. As his career proceeds, Bresson moves further and further away from stories of redemption towards an ever-increasing confidence that the possibility for revelation and mystery reveals itself at all moments and in all things, thus allowing him to acknowledge cruelty and despair without falling into pessimism. 'There is no compromise in Bresson,' writes Tony Pipolo, 'not in *Les Anges du péché* and not in *L'Argent*. The image of the world may seem to have changed between the former and the latter, but this is too simplistic a conclusion.'[9] Later he writes, 'It is no longer only the direction and outcome of the narrative that inevitably ensues from the maxim [of binding people to each other and to objects by looks], but the filmic object itself.' In other words, Pipolo asserts that in Bresson, we have a film-maker with the wisdom to understand that all systems of belief and meaning are transitory, but that the power of the material world to suggest a way to understanding can never disappear, even when it's a backdrop to suicide and murder.

L'Argent

What is *L'Argent*? A warning sign? A contest between the evil of which men are capable and the infallible beauty of reality? A cautionary tale about the dangers of unchecked capitalism? A plea to the world at large to look beyond self-interest? An investigation of the formation of evil?

Why *L'Argent*? Why would a director in his eighties, a moment when most other film-makers attain a peaceful equilibrium, devote his energies to this particular story? Why would an artist who has, in Durgnat's words, remained within the 'sacred sphere', take a polemical late Tolstoy story (after a career devoted to Dostoevsky) and all but strip it of its redemptive second half?

L'Argent is a film whose every instant feels so utterly *alive* that it would be hopelessly reductive to boil it down to a trajectory or set of trajectories, whether thematic or formal. It is easily the fleetest of Bresson's films, almost rocketing past its multiple characters and locations during its brief running time. For the first time, Bresson has set his hero down in the centre of ongoing action, rather than engineered the action around him. And also for the first time, the hero remains an enigma from start to finish. But in fact, we can't know Yvon in the way that we come to know Fontaine or Michel (from a respectful distance), because he can only be a cog in the machinery of this story, cast aside by the virus of usury and self-protection whose progress it charts. Paradoxically, it *is* his story by virtue of his diminishment. Does Bresson suspend the possibility of redemption for Yvon? Not exactly. But by shifting the focus from his hero to the forces that overpower him, the difficulty of attaining redemption is given more of a place than redemption itself. What is it, precisely, that constitutes this difficulty?

If there's one thematic strand that Bresson pulls from the fabric of Tolstoy's novella, it's the opposition of city and country, the cold, man-made functionality of the former versus the natural, oxygenated simplicity and wonder of the latter. But whereas in Tolstoy that opposition develops into an intense hatred of the city and all that it stands for, in Bresson it remains an opposition and nothing more: the plain fact of *things*, both manufactured and organic, and the way people behave around them speak for themselves.

L'Argent opens with a shot of a cash machine's metal door gliding shut after an unseen transaction, over which the credits roll. Once the door closes, the reflection of a bus runs across the cold steel, accompanied by the sound of the motor. But then, even though the sound of passing traffic continues on the soundtrack, the only thing we see reflected on the door is a solid white streak. An apparently simple image is not so simple after all. Why would Bresson go to the trouble of filming the reflection of a bus passing and then leaving nothing but a white streak in the image, while continuing with the sounds of passing cars? And, since we're obviously on a commercial street, where are the sounds of footsteps, the chatter of passing people, and the odd, incidental sounds that fill any cityscape (sirens, beeping horns, clanging objects, etc.)?

Close analysis is often scorned by regular cinemagoers, for the simple reason that it prompts its own way of looking at a film, miles from the experience of just sitting and watching a movie. More often than not, analysis leans on metaphor and interpretation, the pursuit of interlocking patterns, a mechanical process at work behind the film that has next to nothing to do with the way that an artist proceeds when he or she is producing something interesting. The physical shock of Bresson forces you into another way of thinking.

On the previous occasions when Bresson has filmed cityscapes (*Pickpocket, Une Femme douce, Four Nights of a Dreamer, The Devil, Probably*), there is rarely any chatter on the soundtrack, nor are there many stray sounds: our ears become quickly tuned to the subtly disquieting sound of cars in motion. It has a great deal to do with his desire to focus the audience's attention (which he shares with Hitchcock) through repetition and patterning. Throughout *L'Argent*'s first half, the sound of traffic provides a sensorial bridge between scenes. What many other film-makers choose to do with images, Bresson does with his soundtrack – he often either fades down from one sound and into another, or executes a sonic 'dissolve'. But more to the point, a central fact of Bresson's art, beginning with *A Man Escaped*, is the sense of action as an uninterrupted flow, largely accomplished by bridging sequences through sound. This practice became even more refined after *Une Femme douce*, Bresson's first film in colour, since he decided that colour dissolves looked artificial and wrong.

Visually, on a shot-by-shot basis, Bresson likes to imprint a singularized action on a given space, like a charcoal line on a blank sheet of paper. The body is either traced in its stillness, or draws itself across the screen in a quick, decisive movement. When one discusses 'rhythm' in Bresson, it's closer to the idea of rhythm in painting, much more than a question of 'pace', the actual rhythm of action, as in a film by Scorsese or

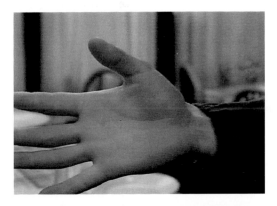

The café scuffle; Martin Balsam's 'fall' in *Psycho*

Coppola, or of shot length, as in Antonioni. In Bresson, and this is a trait that he shares with Hitchcock, the length of a shot has less to do with tempo than it does with sensorial emphasis: it's never a question of a *character* simply living a moment in time, as it is in most films, but the way *one* (i.e. Bresson) would experience the *feeling* of living such a moment. The shot of Yvon's hand as it releases the waiter's arm during the scuffle in the café has a family resemblance to the shot of Martin Balsam 'falling' down the stairs in *Psycho* – both are a-temporal, disjointed from any reasonable space–time continuum, and oriented around a particular sensation. The difference is that Hitchcock is strictly functional, never more so than in Balsam's murder scene, which produces a bizarre

funhouse effect that seems completely unintended. In Bresson, the texture, the light, the aura of the moment, the sense of depth produced through sound all come into play. It's not just people who are bound to objects in Bresson; rather, *everything is bound to everything else*, and the focal point becomes the absolute acuity of perception itself. This is not lost on the majority of writers who have tackled Bresson either critically or theoretically, but it's always posited as a matter of ethics, or morality, or spirituality. There's no denying the aptness of such claims, but they tend to detract from the aesthetic excitement and *sensual* impact of Bresson's art.

One could neatly sum up the opening by stating that Bresson is digging right into the fact of money, the world around it reflected by and

A family dynamic described within seconds

sounded against the steel barrier that keeps it protected. But such a summary ignores the surprise of the cold steel, the sudden excitement of a decisive image, and the magnetizing power of the world around us.

The action of the film proper begins with the opening of a door, the first of many in the film and a constant motif throughout Bresson's cinema ('Doors opening and closing are magnificent,' Bresson told Ciment, 'the way they point to unsolved mysteries').[10] Norbert, the film's equivalent of Tolstoy's Mitya, enters his father's study to ask for his allowance and then for an advance on the following week. Norbert (Marc Ernest Fourneau) is a porcelain-skinned boy with large, liquid eyes, and a limpid gaze – a perfect bourgeois innocent. His father, far from the monstrous tyrant of Tolstoy's story, has the self-important air of a banker turning down a loan. Norbert appeals to his mother, a chic creature who obviously defines herself by her looks. Anyone who complains about the lack of acting in Bresson should take careful note of such a scene, in which a whole family dynamic is described within seconds, with a minimum of screen time and detail: preoccupied parents who live in cold luxury and maintain an even emotional tone (dictated by the father) that they're not used to having disturbed; a boy who feels that he's owed whatever he wants but has enough sensitivity about him to quietly defer to his parents. It's a world away from Tolstoy, carefully observant where he is slyly judgemental, and it's a good lesson in how much most film-makers fail to leave out of a scene, obscuring the essential details that are already there.

When Norbert's father hands him the money for one week's allowance, Bresson shoots the bills in close-up – the exchange of money will be shot in close-up more or less throughout the entire film. One could say that money in this film is a little like the parasite that gets transferred from one character to another via sexual contact in David Cronenberg's *Shivers* (1974). But because of the equanimity that Bresson brings to the filming of all objects, money is never imbued with a sense of evil in *L'Argent*. Bresson is filming a man-made dilemma, and any supernatural or divine influence on events can only be inferred through an interpretation of their overall pattern. After asking his mother for the money, Norbert gets on the phone with his friend Martial (Makhin), and slams it down

(Bresson carefully records the decaying ring) as he walks out the door and hops on his mobilette. Here, Bresson executes a sonic fade-out as Norbert rides away, something he will repeat continually throughout the film.

We begin the scene at Martial's house with a close-up of a watch, which Norbert intends to pawn. The boy who plays Martial is a fair-haired, dark-eyed, proto-male model type, with a sybaritic posture and the hint of an ever-present smirk creasing the corner of his mouth. Thus far, Martial is the character who corresponds most closely to his literary prototype, with the crucial difference that he does not appear to be a wastrel. In his *Film Comment* piece on *The Devil, Probably*, Olivier Assayas refers to the 'timeless bohemia' that Bresson created for that film, with its scenes of hippies strumming their guitars on the banks of the Seine.[11] In *L'Argent*, Bresson performs a similarly abstract operation on an entirely new generation of young people. 'Perhaps you recall that at [the time of *The Devil, Probably*] quite a few young people were burning themselves alive,' Bresson told Ciment. 'Not any more. The present generation is not remotely interested in that. Very odd. To them it's all normal. They belong to an era in which the fact that we are ruining this earth of ours is not shocking.'[12] Bresson is of course referring to a cross-cultural phenomenon that anyone who lived through the 1980s should be able to name easily enough – young fogeys, les jeunes cadres dynamiques, yuppies. Just as in *The Devil, Probably*, only through even more minimal means, he is representing a generational formulation of the world rather than its iconography – Bresson is far removed from the mass cultural preoccupation with labels, styles, 'events'. And his dramaturgical form, as always, has a distinctly nineteenth-century flavour. What is completely up to the minute is the unconscious tunnel vision, the instantly conveyed feeling that an unfulfilled material need requires immediate action. And Bresson gets the two yuppie prototypes perfectly: the Martial type, completely mercenary, and the Norbert type, the innocent who takes marching orders in wide-eyed silence. The evolution from the student artists in *Four Nights of a Dreamer* to the unkempt long-haired lost children of *The Devil, Probably* to the clean-cut, well-dressed bourgeois types of *L'Argent* is striking: what other modern film-maker has been more sensitive to the youth around him?

There's always a great beauty to the handling of objects in Bresson's cinema, with careful attention to weight and volume, and a slowness that gives the action a clarity resembling the ceremonial handling of bread and wine in the preparation of the host (perhaps another reason that Bresson's cinema is often tagged as religious). Bresson carefully films the action of Martial opening a book, taking a 500-franc bill out and handing it to Norbert (in a match cut) to hold up to the light ('Pas mal,' says Norbert, like a kid who's seen too many gangster movies trying to impress his cooler friend), so similar to Michel's practice scenes in *Pickpocket* or Fontaine's handling of the spoon in *A Man Escaped*. This is followed by a curious little exchange, in which Norbert leafs through a book of nudes. Martial peers over his shoulder and says, 'The body is beautiful.' The exchange originates in Tolstoy's novella, in Makhin's references to his beautiful girlfriend, which provides the whole motivation for going to a photo shop and buying a frame in the first place. What counts here is the sense of

The innocent Norbert taking instructions from the sybaritic Martial

The semi-dignified, squarish shopkeeper

detachment, the feeling that Martial is a salesman whispering the words in Norbert's ear, urging him to make a purchase.

Martial picks up his helmet, and we hear the sound of a mobilette motor fading up as Bresson cuts to Norbert and Martial pulling up in front of the photography shop. This type of sound bridge – bringing up the sound from the following scene – is a familiar device in current commercial cinema. Martin Scorsese probably started the practice in American cinema with *Raging Bull* (1980), a vastly influential film (particularly on sound design) and interestingly, the closest the director has ever gotten to Bresson. To go back and experience this practice in a Bresson film is a little startling: odd that something that now seems so completely industrial can feel so artisinal. The exchange in the photography shop (which is pretty bare bones for an upscale neighbourhood in 1980s Paris) is very close to Tolstoy, complete with Martial playing it cool by daring the woman to hold the bill up to the light. But again, the proprietress played by Béatrice Tabourin, far from the usurious hag in the novella, is quiet, erect-postured, all-business, gently frowning in the face of two kids possibly trying to put one over on her: 'You must be joking,' she says when Martial asks if there's a student discount.

'Imbecile!' screams a man's voice, followed by a cut to a close-up of a man's hands examining the bill against the light. It's the woman's husband (Didier Baussy), who has just the right semi-dignified, squarish look for a shopkeeper (the blue blazer and open-collared white shirt are perfect). The original scene in the Tolstoy is a screaming match, but Bresson's version is a little war of accusations and counter-accusations over who has accepted more counterfeit money. Which gets us into an odd area. Had any other director made this film, the scene would probably have had the sloppy, knock-down drag-out spirit of the corresponding Tolstoy scene. So is the fact that it plays as something quite different in Bresson's hands solely attributable to his unique approach to performance style? Can we really say with confidence, as many of his admirers do, that we're looking at the 'essential' version of an emotion that would be 'embellished with acting' in anyone else's hands? Or does Bresson have an essentially quietist temperament that determines not only his working method with actors but also his conception of violence between people? This is precisely the kind of 'issue' that comes up constantly in relation to Bresson – his champions see an essential version of reality while his detractors see a muffling of it. At the risk of sounding equivocal, I would say that the truth lies somewhere in between. Every film-maker has his or her own predilections, gravitating toward favourite milieux or forms of interaction. Somehow, since Bresson's own style and sensibility colours so much more of his film-making process than is the norm, critical concentration shifts to what's missing and away from what's there. I think that Bresson is temperamentally inclined to favour interactions in which emotion is latent, or imminent – when physical violence arrives, it's a quick explosion. But I also think that his way of working with his actors sometimes results in a niggling uncertainty over exactly what one is watching. In other words, there are times in Bresson's cinema when the gap between the action that's inferred and the action that we're really watching gets pretty wide. It's a particular type of problem that doesn't turn up anywhere else in cinema, except in the work of film-makers whose specific aim is to court ambiguity. But since 99 per cent of Bresson's cinema is *completely* clear, it's an odd thing to worry about. Every great film-maker has a 'weak spot', a counterweight to the relentless internal focus required to organize a vision, particularly a vision of true gravity. For Tarkovsky, it's a sort of glassy thickness that invades the action, especially in his later work. For Welles, it's an after-effect of hammy bravado. In fact, to paraphrase Mr Bernstein in *Citizen Kane*, it's easy to deflate any artist, if all you want to do is deflate him.

'I'll pass them on,' says the husband. And this is followed by one of the most beautiful cuts in all of Bresson, to the shot of a man's red-gloved hands capping an oil delivery pipe that sits in a box built into the side of a building. The sheer, breathable tactility of objects in Bresson is often so great that it's startling. Few film-makers allow the actual *identity* of material objects to figure into their scheme of things, beyond the fulfilment of a purely functional role in the narrative. When it does happen at all, it's fitfully, as in Huston's films. There is a wonderful attention paid to objects in the work of the best Portuguese film-makers (Oliveira, Boehtelo, Monteiro) and the new films from Kazakhstan by Omirbaev, Karakulov. The Portuguese films, Oliveira's in particular, have the feel of nineteenth-century pageants acted out amongst friends: the creaking of wooden floors, the sound of dialogue spoken in small echoing rooms or tiny cave-like openings contribute to the feeling of resonant pastness. The Kazakh films are even closer to Bresson with their careful organization of objects in shallow space (the scene of the mother uncovering the prayer amulet in Karakulov's *Last Holiday* (1997) is right out of late Bresson, only more hypnotically fixated on the duration of the event), but the effect is more muted: Omirbaev and Karakulov are both interested in cultivating the delicate, ephemeral side of living in material reality. Whereas in Bresson the pungency of objects always feels like the result of decisive action, the seizing of an instant of perception.

Consider the following scene. The angle of the camera (unlike his fellow 'transcendental' film-maker Ozu, Bresson rarely shoots frontally, apart from faces in close-up), which catches the dimensions and density of each object in Philippe d'Agostini's even but gently sculpting light. The workman's pose, the man's body in dark-green coveralls down on one knee in the corner of the frame, leaning into the task. The vibrant red of the gloves. The sight of human hands caught in the midst of workmanlike absorption. The tan box built into the worn, mildewed side of the building. The echo of metal reverberating against stone and concrete

The sheer, breathable
tactility of objects

when he caps the metal end of the hose. Another match cut as the man
gets up and pulls the lever to automatically re-coil the hose back into its
shaft on the back of his truck – a hard, snaking sound. The gloves pulled
off and the man putting his leg up to balance his pad as he writes out a
receipt, over the sudden presence of traffic noise on the soundtrack.
Finally, the man's face revealed to us as he walks into the photography
shop and unknowingly receives the counterfeit bills that have been
accumulating there during the last few days.

The wonder of this scene, a small but indelible smudge of vibrant,
present-tense aliveness, is deepened even further by the realization that it
comprises our introduction to a character whose life is about to take a turn
for the worse. A rarity in film: it's a scene that involves the actual tasks and
materials of a job, moreover a job as a human activity rather than as an
exchange of labour for capital. The sudden move from characters plotting
their malignant intentions to the pawn going about his daily activity is a
familiar one in literature and in movies, but the scene is so fresh that
Bresson could have invented it. He does not introduce us to this man
through his face. Rather, he introduces us to him through what he does,
not in the general sense (he might have shown him driving his truck or
walking into the shop with the bill in hand, to *signify* simply that he's an
oilman) but in the specific sense: these are the tasks that he performs that
make up a good portion of his life, and that are about to disappear from
that life for good.

A character introduced to us through his body as he works

It's also typical of Bresson that the moment is completely unassuming, so absorbed in physical detail that it doesn't announce itself as part of any grand design. But of course it is: a man who we won't ever really know, who we can't ever really know because he is seen (and comes to see himself) exclusively as a small part of some vast machinery, is appropriately introduced to us not through his face but through his body as he works. It's a doubly appropriate introduction because what he does with his hands is taken away from him along with everything else: those hands will soon be used to destroy. But once again, it's unassuming.

Yvon Targe (Christian Patey) hands the bill to a white-coated assistant, who we will soon know as Lucien/Vasily and who is on familiar terms with the oilman (they greet each other with the familiar 'Salut!'). He then receives the counterfeit money (again, in close-up) from the proprietor. Yvon cuts an interesting figure: big-bodied, porcelain-skinned, with a face that seems childish and yet stonelike, and a demeanour that's slightly opaque, perhaps uncomprehending. He doesn't exactly look like a manual labourer, but he emanates a hurt, stubborn, reactive approach to life that fits the role. Unlike his literary counterpart Ivan Mironov, Yvon has no usurious motives: he's not doubling the price of firewood and selling it to unwitting city-dwellers. Nor does he have the mental wherewithal to find some contemporary equivalent to horse thievery. He's a fuel vendor, strictly a company man. When Yvon goes to a café in the next scene and unwittingly passes on the counterfeit bills, he is called on it

The beginning of Yvon's troubles

Lucien lies to the police; forever framed in doorways, a vision in the act of de-materialising

– he quietly pulls one note after another out of his billfold ('This one?…This one?…'), only to be met with a flat no by the waiter. As in the story, it's the fact that the waiter (rather than the barkeep) insists on keeping the bills and pressing charges that enrages Ivan Mironov/Yvon. Yvon's outrage is rendered through a close-up of his hand grabbing the waiter's arm and then releasing it, Bresson holding on the splayed hand for just a moment (with its gorgeous light devoted to sculpting and defining the hand in space, the shot is quite close to the hand positioned against the sky in Godard's *Nouvelle Vague* [1990]), and ending with a cut to the man's torso and legs knocking into the table before he pulls himself out of the frame. We hear the sound of a siren as the tablecloth falls away.

The scene which follows marks our proper introduction to Vasily/Lucien (Vincent Risterucci), who seems only a little older than Norbert and Martial. In a way his features appear even more unformed than Norbert's – a gaze that seems more knowing but just as impressionable, an outsized jaw, a real *prettiness*, which characterizes a lot of the young men in late Bresson, from *Balthazar*'s Gérard on (as opposed to the hollow-eyed, reedy types in *Pickpocket* and *A Man Escaped*). As Lucien lies to the police about Yvon's visit to the shop, he raises his eyebrows, a dead giveaway (and a small plot hole – surely the company records would verify that Yvon had been making regular deliveries to the photo shop). It's interesting that Bresson drops the moment where the proprietor gives Lucien instructions about what to say to the police, which is in his original script – we only see the proprietor walking into the dark-room and then following Lucien out with his hand on his shoulder. The elision might have served a further streamlining of the action, but it also heightens Yvon's feeling of being suddenly thrown through the looking-glass into a world where self-interest is stripped of all appearances and left naked, like the alien America of John Carpenter's *They Live* (1988). 'They're all crazy,' mutters Yvon as he is marched out the door.

If doors figure prominently throughout *L'Argent*, they have a special place in the scenes involving Yvon's young daughter Yvette and his wife Elise (Caroline Lang). In Tolstoy's novella, Ivan Mironov's wife is quickly injected into the action (unsurprisingly, she's a nag who wants him to be a

Elise and Yvette arriving to
support Yvon in court

better earner) without so much as a character sketch, and his children are
only briefly referred to. In Bresson's film, we are given only a precious few
instants with wife and child, but they're strikingly different from the rest
of the film. Bresson never pulls anything fancy with lighting to signal the
metaphorical role of a given character – everything is done with the frame.
More than anyone else in the film, Elise is a *figural* presence – often silent,
caught in a state of quiet desperation (everything falls just outside her
control), and forever framed in doorways, it's as though she's a vision in
the act of de-materializing. She might be the tall, raven-haired opposite
number of the beautiful fair-haired Jeanne in *Pickpocket*, a similarly figural
presence in the process of *materializing* before Michel's eyes. There's a
slightly ungainly quality to Lang, a sense that she doesn't quite know what
to do with her hands. She is dishevelled like Marika Green as Jeanne in
Pickpocket. When Yvon comes home after his ordeal with the police, the
door opens before his key enters the lock and little Yvette appears, a quick
brushstroke of sloppy childish affection. Bresson then jumps to Elise
appearing and standing in a threshold. Before she crosses the room to
finish preparing dinner at the sink, she suggests to Yvon, his head in his
hands, that they consult a lawyer. That brief encounter is also framed
through a doorway, as is the appearance of Elise carrying Yvette in her
arms in the scene that follows, Yvon's day in court. As in the novella, the
charges are dropped but he's warned not to besmirch the names of
upstanding citizens in the future.

'I couldn't go back on my statement,' says the proprietor in the hallway outside of the courtroom, to which his wife responds, 'I just can't forget the way those boys hoodwinked me.' As opposed to Tolstoy's string of grandiose psychic displacements, this sudden convocation of the conspiratorial trio (they can't wait to start justifying themselves) is characterized by its straightforward defensiveness, pettiness. 'Lucien was marvellous,' says the proprietor, before he puts a few bills in his assistant's pocket and murmurs in his ear, 'Go get that suit you wanted.' Bresson frames the trio through windowpanes as they walk across the courtyard, over the sound of a mobilette engine buzzing like a mosquito. He shifts to a frontal angle on Lucien as he walks into the shop (it feels like one unbroken movement), puts on his white coat and steps into the dark-room. 'What's the sentence for perjury?' he asks as he stands in the brownish darkness by the red light, and when he's told not to worry, he simply mutters, 'I get it.' An idea of the world has taken shape in Lucien's mind, and the spectacle is all the more forceful because it occurs through action only, without accents or editorial embellishments. Lucien, the broad-shouldered quick-study, is the first of three innocents who will be hardened during the course of this film.

Yvon parks his truck for the last time and walks to Elise, who is positioned oddly, leaning her back with apparent discomfort but presumed nonchalance against the side of a metal gate. This is the obsessive side of Bresson ('mulish', as Farber puts it), pinning an actor into a stance that is clearly set up in order to get a consistency and through-line in the film's action (once again, she's placed at a threshold). This unintentionally comical imitation of someone supposedly resting their body against a door is a reminder of how uncommon it is to see moments of relaxation in Bresson. There is uncomfortable rest (*Diary of a Country Priest, Mouchette*), sloth (*Au Hasard, Balthazar*), lethargy and depletion (*The Devil, Probably*), but in each case there is also tension, ready to spring the character up out of a prone position. It's directly connected to a desire for the film to play as one unbroken movement.

A 35mm still camera, resting on a white, shadowed platform – a consumer object about to be purchased. More money, some of it going directly into Lucien's pocket, which marks the beginning of his career as a self-righteous criminal. The white-collar customer who buys the camera remembers that the price had been lower when he'd seen it in the window the day before. Lucien shrugs it off, using his calm, seemingly guileless voice (we only see him from behind) as effectively as he did with the police and then in court. Here is another sound/image compound devoted to a ravishing handling of objects: carefully taking the empty Fuji box from behind the counter, pulling the phony price tag off the camera ('Don't bother,' says the customer) – a sound that Bresson gives a super-real fullness (you can just picture him with his Nagra, doing take after take of stickers being ripped off of metal) – wrapping the strap around the camera and placing it inside, and then Lucien's hand moving slowly and deliberately to the register, delicately extending a finger that opens the cash drawer. Every step in a brief, apparently inconsequential action is given thought, attention and rigorous concentration.

Once the customer leaves, Lucien pockets the money and writes the real price in the ledger. He returns to the dark-room as he sees the owners walking back into the store. The husband enters the dark-room with two conflicting price tags in his hand (how did he have time to get them? did he run into the customer in the street?). His heart suddenly overflowing with 'generosity', he explains to Lucien that he won't prosecute him but that he's going to have to let his faithful employee go. As Lucien leaves the store he's met by two friends, obviously less affluent than Martial and Norbert, and shows them the duplicate keys to the shop that he's made.

Just as in Tolstoy's novella, the proprietress spots Norbert and Martial in the street, Martial makes an ugly face at her as he rides away on his mobilette, and she meets with the religious instructor of the Lycée, who subsequently shames Norbert in class. But unlike the novella, there is no hint of power hunger and self-righteousness in the religious instructor – aside from the archaic pedagogical cruelty of shaming a student before his peers, he's a neutral figure. Again, a minor question, and one that's been there since *Les Dames du Bois de Boulogne* (1945): when Bresson leaves one of these decidedly nineteenth-century details in his narrative, is it

Norbert and Martial riding
their mobillettes

meant to be taken only as a pure plot development or as an idiosyncratic
character choice?

'The religious instructor will probably tell your father. Whatever
happens, deny everything.' This is a mother speaking to her son. The
compliant, wide-eyed Norbert watches his mother walk out the door, and
Bresson follows the chic creature as she strides into the photo shop. 'Now
let's put this absurd story to rest,' she tells the proprietress as she passes
her an envelope full of cash: a close-up of her hand as she pulls the
envelope out of her purse and carefully lays it on the counter. She gets her
assurance that Norbert's name won't be mentioned. We return to the
apartment, where the familial habit of everyday duplicity is repeated with
the father, presumably on his way to see the religious instructor. 'You stay
here,' he instructs Norbert. 'This is so stupid,' he adds as he walks into the
elevator, and his son compliantly closes the door behind him. In Bresson's
original script, the conflict between the father and the instructor was
retained from Tolstoy's novella (which accounts for the urgency of the
mother's request that Norbert deny what happened). But in these two
scenes of a son watching his parents walk out the door to cover for him
when they are actually maintaining their own self-interest, the insight is as
delicate as Tolstoy's revelation of the Tsar's distance from his own
humanity. Just as in the previous instance with Lucien only even more
forcefully, Bresson is showing us the formation of cynicism in a young
mind in the most lifelike way: unconsciously, strictly through action. This is

the last we will see of this boy, who is denied the redemptive sense of purpose and reconciliation with his father that his counterpart gets at the end of the novella. In our last glimpse of him, Norbert is staying obediently behind, watching as his father enacts his self-interested perversion of moral purpose, a turning point in his adolescent study of everyday adult life. In its own way, the scene is just as hurtful as the violence that will follow. Only here, the violence is being done, silently, to a young soul.

We return to Yvon, and just as Bresson explained it to Ciment, he follows Yvon's footsteps as he walks down the Grands Boulevards and takes a seat at a café. In fact, he deliberately mingles Yvon's footsteps with

The formation of cynicism in a young mind

that of a woman walking in the same direction and then with people walking in the opposite direction, a folkway perceived as a multitude of possible perceptual paths to follow, a flurry of motion made up of individuals staking out their own trajectory. How does it feel to walk down the Grand Boulevards, Bresson wonders? As always, the orientation is place-specific rather than situation- or mood-oriented. How does it feel to walk down *this* particular street, to sit on *this* chair in *this* room, to perform *this* action? It's never a question of how it feels for this or that particular character, but simply how it feels. In an attempt to nail down the manner in which urban life figures into Hitchcock's films, Fredric Jameson has written that the definition

must avoid an aesthetic of personal expression, as when I try to render *my* New York by evoking the smooth rising and dipping of cars sweeping at fixed distances from one another down the great north-south avenues of Manhattan, or *my* Paris as the springy impact of a French vehicle on the cobbled section of a boulevard, the new humming of the tires on its paving stones.[13]

Which is, of course, *precisely* what Bresson does at any given moment, and which defines perfectly the difference between his work and that of Hitchcock, the film-maker to whom he has so often been compared.

Yvon is met by a friend, from whom he wants to borrow money. The friend refuses, but makes him a business proposition and ushers him inside the restaurant, into the back room behind the bar. At which point we get a close-up of a woman's legs lounging on a couch, clad in only a pair of panties (another commodity). She's reading a magazine. A man's hand enters the frame, pulls the magazine away and gives her a slap on the ass. She moves off the couch. It's an exchange right out of Phil Karlson or Don Siegel, and a rather charming example of just how wide the gap can be between the things that Bresson is tuned into (contemporary youth) and the things that he doesn't seem to think about at all, content to draw from his stockpile of film memories (modern criminality). All the same, the lack of up-to-dateness counts for less than the brutal dryness of the action, the mindless compliance, and above all the percussive rhythm of the cut. Yvon is summoned to the back room as the woman walks out to the bar to have a drink with her friend (how did she get dressed so fast? another elision?). Yvon is shown a map with an escape route – he's going to drive the getaway car for a team of bank robbers, and Bresson gives us a close-up of the pen tracing the escape route across a map of Paris. Yvon walks back outside to his table, takes another sip of his drink and leaves. His last moment of home life is barely more than a glimpse. It's morning. He kisses his daughter goodbye as she lies in bed, downs his coffee and shoots out the door, his wife once more framed in the doorway, calling after him to tell her what's wrong. She gets no answer.

A man is reading the morning paper as he walks up an inclining street. The camera follows him and then rests on a car, behind the wheel of which sits Yvon. This is a fairly common strategy for Bresson – work your way into a scene through a passer-by (or at least weave him or her into the action), a participant in the overall drama of life, which after all contains or encircles the action. A sudden commotion in the street (people running, police cars), and then back to Yvon, who's obviously gotten more than he bargained for. The man with the paper is still walking, and when he sees a line of armed cops crouched behind a car, he starts running. The robbery has obviously gone awry – one of the robbers is holding a woman hostage (in long shot). A gun is fired, which we hear over a shot of Yvon sitting behind the wheel. His hand turns the ignition key – a whistle blows. A cop car backs up the street and when it pulls up next to Yvon, he takes off. A chase ensues, and Yvon cracks up his car.

If there's a weak section in *L'Argent*, it's this little criminal interlude. Perhaps for the very first time in Bresson, the action feels *movie-ish*. Every plot point in these scenes, from the hookers in the back room to the I-can't-lend-you-any-money-but-I've-got-a-proposition-for-you friend (even though it conforms with the film's overall theme); the stoic husband who can't tell his wife where he's going to the tense war of nerves at the crime scene; and the final, disastrous decision at the wrong moment to take off, is well-worn material that might have turned up any night of the week on American television in the 70s. Which is not to say that in Bresson's hands

it doesn't feel crisp and alive. The sombre, de-glamourized tenor of the heist and car chase – very workmanlike, no flash or bravado – is perfect. But the premise remains clichéd. Bresson's films have nothing to do with the familiar critical idea of 'enlivening familiar material'. If that seems to be the case with *A Man Escaped* and *Pickpocket*, it's because their milieux and plot lines overlap with generic concerns – they certainly don't partake of them. In this interlude, however, Bresson takes a pretty familiar route to get his hero in prison. Apart from some of the poison pen post-war stereotypes in *Diary of a Country Priest* – which, as Frédéric Bonnaud has so perceptively pointed out, are alarmingly close to Clouzot – the only similar failure of imagination in Bresson's œuvre is the unfeeling

The criminal interlude

psychiatrist in *The Devil, Probably*, a modern cliché if ever there was one (at least in French cinema – the psychiatrist in Truffaut's *The Woman Next Door* [1981] is an unshaved wreck, and psychoanalysts are easy targets in two comedies, Raul Ruiz's *Généalogies d'un crime* [1997] and Danièle Dubroux's *Le Journal du séducteur* [1995]). Film-maker Mark Rappaport has perceived a similar problem in André Téchiné's extraordinary *Les Voleurs* (1996), in which he claims that the weakest scene is the only one that deals with actual criminal activity, a car heist that goes wrong; Jonathan Rosenbaum has identified the same problem in Leos Carax's *Mauvais Sang* (1986). Although I would dispute the claim in regard to the Téchiné (the scene looks to me like a poetic wonder), there is a strong sense of creative gear-shifting in all three (French) films, from tough, cogent observations of contemporary life to generic plot machinery and then back again, in order to get the film from one place to another.

Elise is sitting in the police station reading the paper, a black shawl draped over her shoulders. She's obviously been there for some time. She appeals to the desk sergeant, who leaves his post and comes back with the information that Yvon is in custody and that it's unlikely she'll be able to communicate with him until his court date. Bresson cuts back to the cop looking at her as she sits forlornly in the waiting room, and the ominous words 'The Court!' are heard on the soundtrack. Bresson opens the next scene with the red of the magistrates' robes flooding the frame as Yvon is brought into the room. He's found guilty and, due to mitigating circumstances he's given the minimum, three years. Bresson doesn't reveal Elise sitting in the gallery until the end of the scene: Yvon glances back at her as he is walked out of the courtroom. She leaves the court and, framed once more through a doorway, picks up Yvette and carries her away.

Doors become a full-blown presence once Yvon arrives in prison, and a very distinctive one at that: disruptive, regulatory, determining the rhythm and the feel of existence itself. Bresson originally wanted surveillance cameras and televisions to be a motif in the prison scenes, but for whatever reason he dropped the idea: the feeling of containment is so powerful in this section of the film that constant surveillance is a given.

Yvon's second day in court

Yvon's arrival in prison is signalled by a blue corrections bus backing into the frame (the sound of the bus hissing to a stop, the colour blue suddenly filling the frame), the door opening and the officers inside removing all the baggage first, then the prisoners who belong to the baggage, of whom Yvon is second. The bus door closes, the prisoners enter their new home and the steel door clangs shut behind them.

Bresson then takes us back to the photo shop, and slowly fades up (from the omnipresent buzz of traffic) the sound of a ringing alarm, causing the owners to sprint back in from their break and up the stairs, to find an empty safe. It's Lucien and his gang, who are walking quickly down the steps of the metro, Lucien with suitcase in hand. Bresson makes a profoundly idiosyncratic choice here, by holding on the steps over the sound of a train pulling up and then cutting to the platform just as it's pulling out of the station. Did Bresson film the gang of young thieves running to the platform and getting on the train and then cut it? It's an oddly haunting move, managing to embody the feeling of frustrating elusiveness one feels after being robbed, in addition to broadening the film's already impressive array of resonant urban spaces.

Visiting day in prison, which Bresson gets into by blending the sounds of echoing footsteps from the metro with echoing footsteps in the corridors of the prison. A guard walks to Yvon's door and peers in through the eyepiece. He has a visitor. He's in his room, now dressed in his regulation prison garb. The door opens for him. He waits to get buzzed through another metal door, where he is followed by other prisoners down a flight of stairs to a desk where he's handed a number. Yvon walks to a row of wooden partitions, which Bresson frames on an angle, respecting the privacy of each convict. Any good prison film – *White Heat* (1949), *Le Trou* (1960), *The Wrong Man* (1956), *Escape from Alcatraz* (1979) and, of course, *A Man Escaped* – is bound to be heavily involved with procedures, routines. The big difference between this film and Bresson's previous prison films (also including *Les Anges du péché* and *Trial of Joan of Arc*), is the deadening effect of all the procedures combined. As opposed to a Fontaine or a Joan, whose inner fires burn brightly and are inextinguishable, Yvon's soul is snuffed out in prison. Which means that

Arrival in prison; Yvon and Elise's last goodbye

the details are neutral, purely rhythmic; a world away from Fontaine's will to freedom, which gives every moment a terrific immediacy and suspense.

Bresson cross-cuts between Yvon and the silent Elise, keeping both heads carefully in the frame, separated by the plastic partition. These are among the most beautiful shots in the film, in which Patey's and Lang's faces take on an hieratic effect – Patey's smooth, fine-boned features could have been painted by Cranach, while Lang has a gorgeous fullness to her face and a dark lustre that's right out of the Venetian school. After cryptically reminding him that they never quarrelled – the implication is that she's told him she's leaving him – she gets up and walks out, and Bresson cuts to the other side of the partitions, where her departure mingles with the gaggle of voices and the laughter of two animated children in the centre of the frame. It's a good example of the importance of symmetry for Bresson, giving a workable, valid, musical form to any given scene.

A car pulls into the frame, its yellow lights shining in the handsome blue darkness. A man gets out to retrieve some money from a cash machine, and Lucien, now dressed in a suit, is hovering around with his gang. As the man inserts his card and punches in his pin number, Lucien glances over his shoulder. Suddenly an out-of-order sign flashes. 'Ohhh!' exclaims the man (is it Bresson's own voice mimicking a put-upon neurotic Parisian?), and he walks away. Lucien strolls up to the machine and retrieves the card with a pair of tweezers, mindful of the passers-by. He explains to his henchmen that he has to retrieve also the shims that he placed there to trap the card in the first place or else 'the scam won't work again' (he produces a piece of paper with a diagram on it as some kind of proof). He goes back for the shims (a tiny, metallic clanking sound as they come out) and then works his scam, whereupon the metal door opens and the 200-franc bills (in close-up, of course) start pouring out, one after the other. Bresson has always been drawn to such ingenious procedures (the pickpocketing in *Pickpocket,* the whole escape scenario in *A Man Escaped*, the poacher and his traps in *Mouchette*), which signals the anarchic (and vastly underestimated) side of his personality – it actually begins with the disjointed comedy of his first film, *Affaires publiques* (1934). He originally intended Lucien's scam to play a bigger part in the film, closer to Michel's flurry of successes as a pickpocket: in a quick montage, cash machines all over Paris were to be emptied of their loot. We are left with only this brief, almost comically detailed scene. Question: did anyone follow suit and actually rob cash machines in just this manner after seeing *L'Argent*?

As the cash machine door closes, the tall metal gates of the prison open, through which the white mail truck arrives. On a purely technical level, the shot is amazing: the camera pans with the truck as it drives in and frames its back end perfectly as it comes to a stop, without any discernible disturbance in focus. The doors open and the blue mail baskets come out, one of which is promptly dumped on the sorting table inside. It's a very nice moment, with a wonderful mixture of expectation and impending boredom on the faces of the women who do the sorting, followed by a great composition: their arms from all across the table, clad in blue smocks, reaching into the blue basket for a handful of letters to sort. There is a letter from Elise, which we are allowed to read in close-up

Lucien working his cash card scam

Women sorting the prisoners' letters

over the sound of rustling paper. She explains to Yvon that Yvette has died suddenly after having an emergency tracheotomy, and that she had been unable to tell Yvon during their visit. Bresson cuts to the letter on the floor of Yvon's cell, his arm draped over the side of the bed. A hand reaches into the frame and slides the letter across the floor. Yvon's cellmates read it and one of them makes another one of those staccato rhetorical flourishes that crop up like rare flowers in the garden of Bresson's cinema: 'Death frightens us because we love life.' In the scheme of the entire film, it has a terrible irony since the value of life is just about to plummet for Yvon. The men drink a toast and the speechmaker stuffs his bottle back into his mattress. This letter is the most archaic of all the narrative devices in the film, far too musty and formulaic for Tolstoy. But it gets the job done. Unlike his contemporaries, who are preoccupied with, and often get gummed up by, respecting the ambiguous surface of things, Bresson understands that sometimes a blunt instrument is necessary to get the point across and keep the film moving.

Bresson returns to the photo shop and drops in a scene from very late in the novella, after the chain reaction of good deeds is well under way (it's commonly thought that he retained only the first half of the story, but in fact he uses pieces from throughout: at this point, he's mingling Ivan Mironov's actions with Stepan's temperament, and using the post-murder prison episode from the story as a prelude to the murders in the film). A chic blonde woman walks into the photo shop and sits down with the

owners for a chat. They exclaim how badly their business has gone since
the robbery, how awful it is that Lucien robbed them and how easily he
lied in court. 'They say he gives all his money to charity, but you can't
believe everything you hear,' exclaims the woman. The owner goes for the
mail and finds the letter from Lucien with a check for 100,000 francs, and
Bresson highlights the glistening tear stiffly wiped away from the owner's
eye. It's a fascinating moment. First, it's simply dropped into the middle of
the film. Second, given the uniformly brisk pace of Bresson's storytelling,
it carries nothing of the epiphanic spirit that Tolstoy intended. It also feels
faintly unbelievable. However, as a simple contrast to the selfishness that
has characterized most of the people in the film up to this point, it carries
a real jolt. 'Incredible,' exclaims the owner as he wipes the tear away and
looks back at his wife. In this world where self-interest seems so natural
that it's passed on to adolescents like a family heirloom, such a gesture
seems utterly impossible.

Back in the prison mailroom, we get a glimpse of the many returned
letters that Yvon has sent to Elise, which sets up the following scene in the
mess hall, a prison film standard. As everyone sits down to eat and goods
are exchanged under the table, inmates starts looking at Yvon – 'Why is
everyone staring at me?' Which prompts a discussion of women and how
generally faithless they are: 'They're all alike,' answers one of his fellow
prisoners. The news has gotten around that Elise has deserted Yvon. If
this moment also seems a bit movie-ish, the prisoners' actions have a terse,
intrusive brutality that is fairly chilling. 'Who stole her from you?' Which
causes Yvon to swipe the ladle from the passing food cart – Bresson gives
it a sound that resembles a sword being pulled from its sheath – and
prompts the guards to blow the whistle and grab him. First he raises the
ladle, then throws it down and sends it sliding across the stone floor and
bumping into the wall, where it rattles until it stops. Yvon is subsequently
interviewed by the prison officials, one of whom is saddled with a crude
speech as he walks in – 'The man who's never killed is often more
dangerous than the murderer.' Yvon is given forty days in solitary, despite
his denials that he never intended to do real harm, and the decision is
ratified with a signature on an official form. His belongings are gathered

together by a guard in his cell, tied into his blanket, walked through a
metal door and deposited on a shelf.

In the mailroom, one of the sorters pulls a letter from a basket,
which is passed from hand to hand, to the hand of the censor and then
read. It's from Elise, telling Yvon that she wants to make a fresh start and
that they'll never meet again. The paper is folded and placed back in its
envelope with the same care as the camera placed in the box, then marked
'Withheld'.

Outside the door of solitary, the sound of metal scraping against
stone is reprised, only this time it's monotonous, sustained. A guard peers
in before he unlocks the thick wooden door (for anyone used to American
prison films, which feature endless rows and tiers of metal, *L'Argent* offers
an interesting contrast) and walks in. Yvon asks what day it is. The door is
shut again and the scraping continues. The prison doctor comes and
administers two blue pills, which Yvon pretends to swallow, but later spits
out and deposits in a ripped magazine page full of blue valium stuffed in

'Women are all alike' – a prison film standard

his mattress, just like his old cellmate's bottle of booze. Bresson cuts to a pair of dirty feet on a stone floor. Yvon's cellmates are looking out a window at the ambulance that has pulled up below, and one of them, clad only in pyjama bottoms, walks to his bed and kneels. 'I always pray for suicides.'

In the prison hospital, we get a series of details that have a hallucinatory starkness – a monitor, which bleeps throughout the scene; the letter from Elise resting in a tray; the pump of a ventilator moving up and down; Yvon's forearm stretched out on the white bedding, a wondrous image devoted to rendering the beauty of Patey's dark skin tone; a woman's hand adjusting one of the control knobs on the machine. It's the nurse, who gets up in a deft little match cut to the next shot, which pans over to Yvon. 'Ça va Yvon?' she asks nonchalantly, to this man unable to breathe on his own, let alone speak.

The bleeping gives way to the rustling of papers and Lucien's day in court, where he refuses to accept the authority of law and promises to steal again after he escapes, in order to distribute more money to charity – unlike Tolstoy's Vasily, there is no particular charity that Lucien seems to favour. Bresson also adds an interesting detail by having the judge comment ironically on Lucien's expensive taste in suits. It's a reminder that Lucien's first ill-gotten gains were used for the purchase of a suit.

The blue bus, already backed in place: now it's Lucien's turn. Just as before, the bags come off first; and just like Yvon, Lucien is the second prisoner led off the bus. As he gets off we hear the sound of another vehicle pulling up next to the bus. It's the ambulance, bringing Yvon back from the hospital.

Bresson follows this with the ultimate in his career-long series of hectoring, pretentious speakers, indifferent to their listeners. Yvon's new cellmate paces back and forth with a book in his hands (his finger marking some inspirational passage) as Yvon lays on his bed, pictures of his family pinned to the wall behind him, and quietly listens. The absurdity of society, the impossibility of change, wanting happiness 'on my own terms', and a terrible diatribe against money, 'our false God'. And suddenly, very oddly, he asks Yvon to show him his legs. Yvon lifts up his pant legs and complains of weakness in the knees. The man tells him that it's an after-effect of the valium overdose. The speech is an embodiment of post-60s, purely reactive thinking, the urgency and commitment of the original revolutionary impetus thinned out to unrecognizability by narcissism. What's especially brilliant about this moment is the inclusion of the anti-money sentiments. One might say that they are in accordance with the film's point of view, but the words are meaningless in the face of the terrible fashion in which they're delivered: badgering a man who's just tried to take his own life. What one says in Bresson is completely meaningless; what one does in everything. The sound of a humming floor polisher is heard outside the door. Someone has a message from Lucien for Yvon, to sign up for mass. The pompous cellmate advises him not to, but Yvon is bent on revenge. Outside the door, the convict with the floor polisher disappears down the hall, the humming dissolves into the voice of a priest giving a Latin mass.

Lucien and Yvon at the prison mass

Mass is a makeshift black market: a tape is exchanged for money, coupons are exchanged for a bottle of perfume. Yvon sits next to Lucien, amidst the blue sea of the prison uniforms. 'I'm going to get you out of here,' says Lucien, the hubristic good samaritan, and offers a detailed plan of escape and then a promise of help on the outside. 'I'd rather kill you than leave with you,' says Yvon. When Lucien contends that they're the only ones there with nothing on their respective consciences, Yvon reminds him, 'I'm on your conscience, and don't you forget it.'

The bottom of a closed door and the floor beneath it. The sound of a wailing siren. A line of light. Running feet, shadows in the light. Yvon wakes up and goes to the door. It's Lucien, and they've got him. 'You're avenged without lifting a finger,' says his cellmate. It's interesting to recognize at this point that Bresson has essentially inverted the progress of Tolstoy's Vasily, whose conversion to good deed doer, intimated during the section when he works on the farm, is the result of his prison experience, where he's influenced by Stepan's example, before he successfully escapes. Here, he goes down in flames in every way imaginable – it's unclear whether he's only been captured or actually shot and killed during his escape attempt. 'Someone somewhere cares about you, a relative or a friend,' says the cellmate. Yvon reminds him that he has no one, not even a wife, and gives him the letter from Elise. 'Don't worry, you'll be back in shape in no time.' When Yvon starts pounding his fists against the door, the cellmate gets bored and his kindness suddenly dries up. 'Can't you do that more quietly? You bore me.' Once again, the disparity between the presumed action – pounding fists into a bloody pulp, like Jake La Motta in *Raging Bull* – and the real one – a measured, rhythmic knocking – is great. But as always, it's the observation and perception of the act as it falls within a continuum rather than its messy surface appearance (the rendering of which runs the risk of fakery and audience disbelief, as Bresson has often pointed out in interviews) that Bresson is after. It may feel disconcerting given modern cinema's predilection for sensorial extravagance and the cathartic spectacle of bloodshed. But that's only a matter of fashion. And it's important to remember that Bresson began making films long before the popularity of squibs or Rick Baker special effects, during a time when film-makers and audiences had a very different relationship with images.

There's no doubt that each Bresson film is all of a piece, and it's especially true of *L'Argent*, even though it covers a wider variety of milieux and characters than any of his other films apart from *Au Hasard, Balthazar*. Every event is like a link in a chain, forged from an alloy of many different substances – narrative drive, with an unusually uniform pace; figural and visual harmony between shots, and an accompanying flow of sounds; and most of all, Bresson's supreme sensitivity to the way that actions evolve and affect one another, forcefully apparent in this film. But if it can be said that there is a greatest sequence in Bresson, it may well be the final section of his final film. The entire film leads up to it, of course, but it's no disservice to Bresson to say that he never filmed anything quite so penetrating, so psychologically acute, so disturbingly perched between grace and damnation as the final twenty-three minutes of *L'Argent*.

The Ending

The prison door swings open, and Yvon walks out, his belongings in two canvas bags, one hanging over each shoulder. A group of guards appears, and one of them hands him his release papers. The big outer steel door is opened and we are re-introduced to the sound of traffic. Yvon leaves his prison, reading his papers as he walks before folding them up and putting them in his pocket. He stops at a black door, where he knocks and is promptly let in by a woman, her husband standing behind a desk in the background. Oddly, Bresson cuts to the sign outside: Hôtel Moderne. One might be tempted to consider this an ironic gesture, were it not for the fact that Bresson's proclivity for irony seems close to zero. More likely, it's just a forceful way of marking the spot where a terrible deed is about to occur.

How much time has passed before the following shot, of Yvon walking down the stairs over the body of one of his murder victims? In

The unnamed woman at the heart of the film

fact, it doesn't matter. He goes to a sink to wash his hands, and Bresson cuts to a close overhead angle as the clear water starts running red and then goes clear again. Yvon wraps up his bloody pants and carefully places them in his bag before snapping it shut, fastens his belt buckle, steps behind the counter, opens two drawers and empties them of their cash (again, in close-up). And he's out the door.

The blunt, ultra-direct manner in which Bresson gets into the murders comes as an ice-cold shock. In a movie so devoted to uncovering the tastefully shielded side-effects of institutionalized indifference, through the toughest punch-counter-punch narrative structure, the sudden intrusion of murder kicks the film up to a new, heightened level: every interaction thereafter carries the expectation of a black outcome. But miraculously, nothing changes in the film's tone, in its rhythm, and, most importantly of all, in its position towards Yvon. And that's why there's a big gulf between *L'Argent* and every other film ever made about murder. Bresson's strategy throughout *L'Argent* is not to cultivate or dramatize the abnormality or psychosis buried within society. Rather, he allows society to reflect back on itself, to give a moral accounting of itself. If an employer pays his assistant off for lying in court, the assistant will take the hint and steal from the employer; if a man has his livelihood taken away from him, he's going to resort to making money illegally. The tone isn't pedantic, it's elemental.

Given all the critical energy that's gone into separating Bresson from his contemporaries (which he himself has helped to perpetuate), it's important to remember that *L'Argent* shares certain characteristics with other films made around the same moment, specifically the American melodramas that grew out of the early to mid-70s paranoid conspiracy genre, like *Cutter's Way, Ragtime, Prince of the City* and *True Confessions* (all 1981). Each one of these films traces a social 'malaise' (to use Jimmy Carter's much-maligned phrase) across a wide variety of characters, locations, classes and situations. Unlike Bresson's film, they each avail themselves of that great American instrument, righteous indignation, starting from the supposition that the culture has become hopelessly decadent and finding a situation to dramatize the decadence: it's as though there was a dark cloud of evil hanging over New York and southern

True Confessions; Prince of the City

California. For Bresson, the important thing is working step by step from concrete facts, in both the philosophical and the narrative senses. With all due respect to *Prince of the City* and *True Confessions*, they seem grandiose and hysterical (philosophically – they remain very fine in their particulars) when compared with Bresson's patience, which moves his film onto a more elevated moral plane. If one has been drawn into the film, it's alarming to see the sum total of misfortunes that have befallen Yvon adding up to his complete devaluation of human life coupled with a cynical belief in the ultimate value of money, all the more alarming since Bresson is so specific. He's not saying that unbridled capitalism and the indifference of modern society breed murderers, but rather that the self-interest and indifference that exist today have created conditions that make such a thing possible.

But those are just words on a page. To see Bresson track the evolution of murder purely through unembellished action, the physical world all the while remaining vibrantly, thrillingly alive, is a jolt, and a rejoinder to a good deal of the woozy hypothesizing about modern culture that's currently in print. Gallons of academic ink have been spilled about the allegedly complex involvement of technology-business-language-cultural/gender bias in the process of transforming human life – the bulk of it is so self-enthralled that the unit of the human being is virtually erased amidst all the theorizing. It's bracing to witness Bresson laying out the plain truths of the modern world by returning his medium to the level of pure action. Cinema is of boundless interest to cultural theorists, but as a monolithic cultural phenomenon rather than as an art form. Few of them, as far as I can see, have the imagination to realize that it can be this tough, this demonstrative. Modern art doesn't come any simpler or more devoid of conceptual trickery than *L'Argent*. Under the current Babel-like circumstances in art, its directness feels like a dare.

At this point, we're miles from Tolstoy. *The Forged Coupon* is like a pool of water hardening into a block of ice in the arctic air of mercenary capitalism, then slowly melting under the warmth of a Christian sun. Society in Tolstoy's novella is viewed from a great height, not unlike that of the angels in Wenders' *Wings of Desire* (1987). It's the benevolent, unblinking, all-encompassing viewpoint of Tolstoy himself, spanning his enormous wings over all of Mother Russia, susceptible to transformation by his loving touch. Whereas with Bresson, it's one action at a time, everything happening at eye level, the time frame resolutely human. In Tolstoy's scheme of things, murder is simply the point from which things can not sink any lower, and thus the beginning of the road to redemption. But for Bresson, the compulsion to murder merits its own exploration. The rejection of life versus the acceptance of life: this is the opposition at the core of the final scenes of *L'Argent*.

Colourful toys in a store window, a sad reminder of Yvette – one can just barely see the reflection of Yvon's face. And as Yvon is staring into this window, a small, silver-haired woman in black with a brisk, stoop-shouldered walk crosses his path. He follows her and stops to watch as she walks through the creaking door of the local post office, where she cashes a money order (in the original script, Bresson had included a bit of the theological conversation between Mariya Semenovna and a store owner – unthinkable that he even considered leaving it in). He sees her taking money out of her purse. The camera cuts in closer: the woman's hands rearranging the money and quietly snapping her black purse shut, which summons the sound of rushing water and the sudden – and altogether shocking – entry of greenery, earth and air into the momentum of *L'Argent*. Bresson cuts to the woman crossing a little foot bridge over a river as Yvon follows her in the distance, a nice landscape that looks well-worn, a world away from the manicured dreams of country life that have plagued movies for years. As she walks into her house, she is greeted by her dog. She turns to look at the stranger who's been following her before she closes the door. Yvon turns back. There's a perfect instance of Bresson's musical ear for sound here: when he cuts to the woman looking back and closing the door, he doesn't vary the sound level of the river. The sudden appearance of natural elements in his film is so strong that their sound is not to be adjusted according to camera distance. And rhythmically, the constant rushing of the water breaks wonderfully into the dog's barking at the opening of the next scene.

The dog, who will play a crucial role in the film's penultimate scene, is irritated – there's something wrong. Yvon walks in, and the woman quickly sizes him up. On closer inspection, this plain woman (Sylvie van

Yvon and the woman

den Elsen) has delicate, tiny features that have been careworn into a kind of flat smoothness, her body solidified from a life of never-ending work. Her manner is recessive, compliant, but quietly adept – a woman who has accepted the condition of servitude. Yvon tells her he's hungry but could go without supper, and she instructs him to take a seat. She immediately goes and closes the door to a room where an old man who doesn't even acknowledge her presence is standing. She walks into another room down the hall and tucks a young boy into bed, shutting that door behind her. Then she walks back to the kitchen. It's important to convey the tonal beauty of these scenes in the house, the dominant colours being black, tan, and a blue that often turns up in Van Gogh: tinged with grey, somewhat sombre, yet very much of the earth. The house – simple, unadorned, breathable – is worn with living but lovingly tended to.

'Why did you kill them?' the woman asks Yvon as he eats. By breaking into the next point in the scene this way, Bresson gives the sympathetic viewer another shock. He's followed the rough outlines of Tolstoy's original character in his conception of this magnificent woman, but whereas Mariya Semenovna affects people indirectly through her example, in life as well as in death, and never actually meets her murderer until the moment before he kills her, her counterpart actually engages in spiritual battle with Yvon. He braggingly recounts the details of the murder and the thrill it gave him (words uttered in the story by a post-redemptive Stepan to Makhin) as he eats his soup – 'I hardly took anything...Their bodies revolted me.' 'If I were God, I'd forgive the whole world,' says this small, indomitable woman, sitting across the table from a self-confessed murderer without even blinking. The dog sidles up to Yvon, and he strokes its head with his free hand as he eats. A door slams somewhere in the house and Yvon bolts. The woman reassures him: it's only her brother and sister-in-law coming home. They go up the stairs, where another sister also lives. 'You're good people,' says Yvon. 'I know you won't turn me in.' It's as though he's stolen money or killed a chicken. Outside, police cars cruise down a nearby road.

Morning. The woman's hands withdrawing a yellow porcelain urn from a silver pot of hot water and pouring steaming, rich black coffee into a wide white cup, using her finger for balance. She carefully walks across the grass in her sandals when she is stopped in her tracks by her father (Michel Briguet), the old man previously glimpsed through the doorway, sad-eyed and threadbare – the camera takes a nice lateral path to follow her and pick him up as he blocks her path. He lets her have it for allowing a total stranger spend the night. 'Leave it to me, father,' she says, 'I'll take care of it.' 'Idiot!' Bresson cuts to a close-up of her face, completely guileless, as her father slaps her, and then cuts quickly to the cup tipping and the hot coffee spilling over her hands. This scene serves as an excellent refutation of the lazy, commonly-held idea that Bresson is all about somnambulant, uninflected action. Every detail here is so specific, and every aspect of the film-making is devoted to rendering that specificity: a small woman juggling a preciously guarded inner life with the needs of an overbearing family; a clinging father who treats her like a child; a particular task (carrying breakfast to Yvon) on a particular path of well-trod green grass in early morning light; a slap delivered as a public humiliation and devaluation, somewhat like a nun slapping a disorderly student on the wrists with a ruler; the feeling that the interaction is well-rehearsed, as though this was the nine thousand four hundred and sixty-eighth time this grown woman was 'caught' doing something that disrupted her father's drably habitual order. She simply lets the slap happen and the coffee scald her hands (Bresson and his cinematographer actually catch the sudden sway of the coffee in the cup, the most striking and exacting match cut in the film) before continuing to the stable, where she puts the coffee on the floor by Yvon's side, under her father's watchful eye. When she leaves, he walks back inside with her. Yvon wakes up and takes a sip of coffee, and that's when he spots an axe lying on the floor. We hear the sound of Bach being played on a piano.

A bottle of white wine and a glass rest on top of an upright piano as the father plays. The woman quietly irons laundry in the kitchen (she even irons the folds) while Yvon sits quietly in the corner, stroking the dog's head. Time for her rounds again. She leaves the room to pick up a book from the floor for her nephew, who sits in a wheelchair at a table, and gives him a kiss. She looks in on her father and closes the door. The father stops

playing for a moment to take a sip of wine and then carelessly places it on the very edge of the piano before he starts playing again. The glass falls and the music stops. The woman automatically puts down her ironing and walks back in with a sponge and a dustpan, and the old man simply waits until she's cleaned up his mess and left the room before he starts to play again. No one else in cinema has ever caught the rhythms of an unloving household as perfectly as Bresson does here – everything unsaid, everyone assuming a particular role and taking private pathways through the house to avoid contact, unconscious gestures of hostility that crudely mask a desire for interaction (the dropping of the glass), hyper-attentiveness to every sound and every action (the second the glass drops, he stops playing and she's right there with the sponge), an arrested, childish atmosphere (Yvon must sit in the corner and watch her iron clothes). Psychology may be the last stop on Bresson's aesthetic and moral itinerary, but he certainly betrays a profound understanding of it here – there's a whole biography of a family woven into these brief scenes. When Yvon tells the woman that she should pack up and leave, that her family treats her horribly, she corrects him: 'I can't reach him,' she says of her father, 'he started drinking when my husband died. Then he lost all his pupils. He used to be a kind family man.' It's easy to hear the cries of 'enabler' and 'dysfunctional family', but Bresson gets so deep inside the mechanics of the situation that such labels seem hollow, meaningless. In fact, these moments are so vivid and so specific that one might be tempted to see a self-portrait in there somewhere.

Earth. The woman's thin white legs, feet in black clogs. Her arms press down on a pitchfork, and the tongs cutting through the packed soil carry the same satisfaction as Farber's *Asphalt Jungle* example. She digs in and lifts, and the soil yields potatoes. The woman bends down and gathers them in her lap, then stands up and holds them in her apron. She walks through the door and changes into her sweater as Yvon carries the potatoes to the kitchen. A quick snatch of piano music, and then the father appears. 'Where are you going?' 'I'll be right back,' says the woman as she crosses the footbridge, from the same angle as in the previous scene (Bresson often repeats an angle when he returns to a location, to refamiliarize the audience

with the space). A bit later, Yvon peers out the kitchen window at a lonely vision – the father pacing back and forth in the garden, his hands behind his back, at odds with himself until his daughter's return. Yvon suddenly bolts away and goes upstairs in search of money. Bresson angles into the corner of this tiny room as Yvon riffles through a chest of drawers – how many other film-makers have ever devoted such time and attention to rendering the feel of a small, unprepossessing bedroom in a country house? Interestingly, the sound of the water from the river fades up on the soundtrack here, prefiguring the film's climactic scene.

In town, the woman walks into a bakery, and as she leaves with bread in her arms, two cops are going in. They pass her on either side, like the cops passing Henry Fonda in *The Wrong Man*. She walks past the police cars and out of the frame, and the cops enter the frame with bread in their hands, passing it to their fellow officers in the car – cheeky. But then why else would cops be going into a bakery? They have to eat too.

The sound of water again, and scrubbing. Bresson fixes on a shot of a wheelbarrow outside the back of an old water wheel house, a lonely, forgotten little space that merits his camera's attention – a fence, grass with bare patches, a clump of weeds, moss creeping up the side of the house, a stone wall covered with vines and more weeds, a small patch of sunlight behind the trees above. The woman is doing the washing, scrubbing the clothes over the stone and wringing them dry. Bresson is so keyed into the reality of manual labour in this setting (and in the film on the whole) that one hardly even registers the anachronism – it's immaterial (in fact, a washer-dryer would seem decidedly out of place). 'He hits you,' says Yvon. 'You're a slave. I don't know why you don't throw yourself in the river. Are you expecting a miracle?' The woman stays silent, keeps at her work. And suddenly she answers: 'I expect nothing.'

The sound of the wheelbarrow. And Yvon's hands, in a series of shots, pick fruits off a tree. The lyricism of nature, the leaves in the trees – an old gig in cinema, usually overlit, overly precious. Bresson films it with such delicacy that it might be the first time you've ever seen it in a film. The light is soft, but everything is clearly defined – the fruits with their green crowns, the severely ridged leaves, Yvon's pink hands, the snap as he picks the fruits from their branches, the wind. He collects some in his cupped hands and brings them over to the woman. He gives her one, and she looks Yvon right in the eye as she puts it in her mouth and crunches it between her teeth. Yvon helps her hang her laundry, and Bresson slightly exaggerates the sound of the clothespins clicking on the line. It may be a moment of drudgery, but it's also a moment of kindness, of silently shared confidence between two mistreated human beings enjoying a brief idyll of grace in the natural world.

A worn, unpainted wooden door. The sound of footsteps. All at once, the grooves and scratches in the wood are illuminated by the glowing orange light of a lantern. The door is broken open with an axe, and the lantern slowly illuminates the rooms in the house before Yvon sets it down on the floor. The dog, howling in agitation, frantically runs out of the couple's room as they stand at the threshold, and down the stairs to the body of the father, past Yvon as he walks with the bloodied axe hanging by his side, past the couple now lying dead on the stairs, into the boy's room – he's sitting up in bed sobbing. Yvon walks into the woman's room and screams the same words at her that Stepan does at Mariya Semenovna – 'Ou est l'argent?' 'Where's the money?' The whole sequence – the whole *film* – contracts into these blunt words. But unlike Mariya Semenovna, the woman simply looks at Yvon, and doesn't move. Fear? Expectancy? Grace? Absolution? A placid mirror of Yvon's own debasement? The axe swings back in the air, and Bresson cuts to the dog, who barks ferociously. The axe

slams into a lamp on a side table (in a match cut) and streaks blood on the wallpaper. The small spot that's still illuminated disappears as the light goes out. We hear the sound of running water. The axe is thrown in the river and sinks. And Yvon leans against the doorway of the house in the darkness – it's as though he's staring back into the eyes of the woman he's just slaughtered. It's one of the most ferociously concentrated scenes in cinema, hitting a perfectly sustained chord of upset. And there is a profoundly troubling dimension to these murders that has absolutely nothing to do with Tolstoy's story. The evidence is undeniable that on some level, this woman, who houses a man who has confessed to two entirely gratuitous murders, who feeds him and exchanges confidences with him, and who

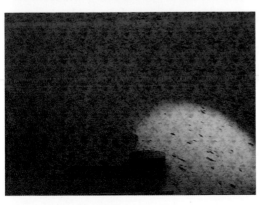

refuses to turn him over to the police or warn her loved ones, is asking to be murdered, putting an end to a life of hardship for herself and her family. It's as though the burden of accepting *so* much is too great. 'I let myself get carried away by my own daydreams,' said Bresson of the process of writing the script for this film, and this is perhaps the oddest, most perverse daydream of all. But it is finally a painfully human desire that Bresson gives us through this woman. And through Yvon. This is indeed psychology, but pitched at such a profound level of experience that the term loses its clinical trappings. Somewhere in that beautiful space between the wind blowing through the trees and the sheets hanging on the line, Yvon and the woman achieve an understanding, two human beings drained of all pretenses, all fantasies, or any semblance of a self-image to hold up to the world for judgement (like Adam and Eve in Bresson's long-cherished *La Genèse*), appearing to one another as questions: prolong a life of misery amidst such natural splendour, or obliterate it?

Truly, there has never been another moment like this in cinema. And there has never been a character like this woman. Or like Yvon. Murder has been a fixture in films since the 20s, and in the last ten or fifteen years, the spectacle of murder has become more than a fixture: it now seems to be a compulsion. Why? Lionel Trilling explored the contemporary fascination with evil in an essay on the then-and-still current unpopularity of the genteel William Dean Howells. For Trilling, the modern condition is characterized by the overvaluation of evil as a power, in response to the bloodlessness of everything around it, resulting in an essentially passive confrontation – 'there is something suspect in making evil the object of, as it were, aesthetic contemplation.' It all finally boils down to the troubling question of 'why we believe, as we do believe, that evil is the very essence of reality'.[14] In a very real way, the omnipresence of murder in cinema, on television, in fiction, in music and in conversation is a kind of guarantee, a shield against an officially sanctioned, commercially infected version of reality that has been unofficially yet widely branded as untrustworthy. Thus the cliché of the 'banality of evil', in which the most violent acts spring from the most seemingly humdrum circumstances. The ultimate example might be John McNaughton's *Henry Portrait of a Serial Killer* (1989), which has a

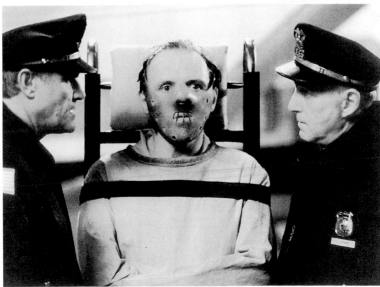

Serial killers: Henry in *Henry Portrait of a Serial Killer* and Hannibal Lecter in *The Silence of the Lambs*

numbing devotion to the idea that masses of disenfranchised individuals are dwelling on the fringes of society, with storehouses of debased instincts and plenty of time to kill, and without the protections of imagination or impulse control. More common (and closer to Trilling's idea) is the serial killer as superhuman, in total possession of his faculties, who offers the terrifying possibility that following his example might just lead the way to total ecstasy. The prototype is, of course, Anthony Hopkins' Hannibal Lecter in Jonathan Demme's film version of *The Silence of the Lambs* (1991). But in that case too, with the extra dimension of class thrown into the mix (Lecter is an upper-middle-class killer with refined tastes who eats the organs of his victims, the insides; while his lower-middle-class counterpart, Buffalo Bill, has a hopelessly banal fixation on the surface, the skin), evil dwells mainly within the lower tier of society. And in each case, murder is signified as an inherently evil act – in McNaughton's case by making it thoroughly banal, thus magnifying its 'believability'. What Bresson does in *L'Argent* is to *separate* evil from reality, to show the circumstantial, human origins of an evil act, without giving us the spectacle of the act itself in which we can supposedly 'implicate' ourselves (another modern cliché). We get something extraordinary from this film, which is the *human dimension* within (and inseparable from) the *action* of murder, followed by the murderer's realization that he has perpetrated evil. During the Son of Sam terror that paralysed New York over twenty years ago, Werner Herzog gave an interview to *Rolling Stone* in which he declared that we must never forget that such a man is not a mad dog but a human being, and that as a human being he still merits respect. It's a hard pill to swallow, but that's exactly what the sympathetic viewer of *L'Argent* must do.

The sound of footsteps, and the door of a café opens. Three men enter in a row, including Yvon and a cop behind him. Yvon sits down and orders a drink. He folds his hands and stares at the floor, downs his cognac, then gets up and walks over to the cop's table. 'I was the one who killed the innkeepers, and I've just murdered a whole family.' One last, very deft ellipsis, as Bresson cuts to a waiter in the other room wiping down a table. He sees people running, but unlike the man reading his morning newspaper during the bank heist stand-off, the waiter heads into the other room to see

what's going on. Bresson shifts outside the café for his final image. A crowd of people has gathered just outside the door, on the left of the frame. Their voices die down, and footsteps are heard. Yvon is led out the door in handcuffs. Even after he's gone, these people, crowded together in darkness, remain still, motionless, craning their necks to look in complete silence – even the ambient sound has dropped away. And we go to black.

It's an unsettling, profoundly ambivalent ending. As Bresson himself has admitted, he did not linger on Yvon's redemption since the rhythm of the film wouldn't allow it. And he's right: given the uniform briskness of *L'Argent*, to linger would be false. Just like Lucien's credit card scam, the father slapping his daughter and each of the murders, this is just another in a chain of actions. And it's finally the neutrality of actions, one leading into the next, that sits at the centre of this film – actions without the helpful accompaniment of words or audio-visual cues to explain them. The final action we see in the film does not belong to Yvon but, properly for a film about a society that disregards him, a group of people huddled together raptly staring at the spectacle of his arrest. Is Bresson condemning them as 'spectators, standing on the sidelines'? I don't think so. It's a supremely logical reaction, but the way that Bresson frames their heads expectantly perched in the darkness, they carry an unmistakable echo of the self-interested, indifferent people who have paraded throughout the film – they are literally trying to *see* this murderer, to feel his presence, to comprehend him and thus surpass their collective habit of self-interestedly glossing over what's before them. Just like every three-dimensional object that passes before Bresson's camera in *L'Argent*, a film in which the physical world is palpable as in no other, they are all distinct and individual in substance. But in another sense they could be absolutely anyone. Anyone.

Postscript

I was in my early twenties the first time I saw *L'Argent*. Even though it wasn't clear to me at the time, its physical immediacy left an indelible impression. I saw the film many times, and never forgot the vision of that pitchfork cutting into the earth, or the sound of those clicking clothespins. As I've grown older, and seen the film many more times under a variety of circumstances, I've come to understand it and all its implications more clearly. But I know that my first instinct, to jump into its sensual details, was right.

While writing this book, America has been engulfed in anguish and fascination with two teenagers named Dylan Klebold and Eric Harris, who walked into their suburban Colorado high school on Hitler's birthday and murdered thirteen people, wounding many others in the process, before they took their own lives in the school library. The Littleton massacre was the fifth such incident in America during the last few years. Exactly one month later, a boy in Georgia brought a gun to school and wounded several students before he surrendered. *L'Argent* is sixteen years old, and we're now into an entirely new generation of kids, as different from the ones in the film as they were from the dishevelled youth of *The Devil, Probably*. Bresson is now a very old man – by some accounts ninety-one, by others ninety-eight – and he's obviously incapable of working again. I'm sure that had he been younger, he would have made a film about these boys who were driven to murder, about their loneliness, their isolation, and the monstrous popular culture that surrounds them, so divorced from the sensual world that he put at the centre of his films. Who else has the patience, the fortitude, the bravery and the sensitivity to help us comprehend *their* humanity, in the same way that he gave us Yvon's humanity? But this is wanting too much from an artist who's given us more than enough already.

Notes

1 David Thomson, *Biographical Dictionary of Film* (New York: Alfred A. Knopf, 1994), p.72.
2 Meyer Schapiro, 'On the Humanity of Abstract Painting', in *On the Humanity of Abstract Painting* (New York: George Braziller, 1995), pp. 16–17.
3 Manny Farber, 'New York Film Festival – 1968', in *Negative Space*, expanded edn (New York: Da Capo Press, 1998), p. 232.
4 Michel Ciment, 'I Seek Not Description but Vision: Robert Bresson on *L'Argent*', trans. Pierre Hodgson, in James Quandt (ed.), *Robert Bresson* (Toronto: Cinémathèque Ontario,1998), pp. 501–6.
5 Tony Pipolo, 'Rules of the Game: On Bresson's *Les Anges du péché*', in Quandt (ed.), *Robert Bresson* , p. 208.
6 Farber, 'John Huston', in Farber, *Negative Space*, p. 35.
7 Raymond Durgnat, 'The Negative Vision of Robert Bresson', in Quandt (ed.), *Robert Bresson*, p. 411.

8 Leo Tolstoy, *The Forged Coupon*, trans. David Patterson (New York and London: W.W. Norton, 1986), p. 92.
9 Pipolo, 'Rules of the Game: On Bresson's *Les Anges du péché*', in Quandt (ed.), *Robert Bresson*, p. 208.
10 Michel Ciment, 'I Seek Not Description but Vision: Robert Bresson on *L'Argent*', in Quandt (ed.), *Robert Bresson*, p. 507.
11 Olivier Assayas, 'The Permanence of the Devil', trans. Kent Jones, *Film Comment,* vol. 35 no. 4, July/August 1999, p. 51.
12 Ciment, 'I Seek Not Description but Vision', in Quandt (ed.), *Robert Bresson*, p. 507.
13 Fredric Jameson, 'Reading Hitchcock', *October,* no. 23, Winter 1982, p. 24.
14 Lionel Trilling, 'William Dean Howells and the Roots of Modern Taste', in *The Opposing Self* (New York and London: Harcourt Brace Jovanovich,1979), p. 89.

Credits

L'Argent

France/Switzerland
1983

Director
Robert Bresson
Producer
Jean-Marc Henchoz
Screenplay
Robert Bresson
Inspired by the story
The False Note by
Leo N. Tolstoy
Directors of Photography
Pasqualino De Santis,
Emmanuel Machuel
Editor
Jean-François Naudon
Art Director
Pierre Guffroy
Music
'Chromatic Fantasy' by
Johann Sebastian Bach,
performed by Michel Briguet

©Marion's Films
Production Companies
A co-production of Marion's
Films/FR3 (Paris)/EOS Films
(Switzerland)
Executive Producer
Antoine Gannage
Associate Producers
Jean-Pierre Basté, Patricia
Moraz
**Production
Administrators**
Simone Tabarly, Catherine
Huhardeaux, Françoise
Thouvenot
Unit Manager
Richard Dupuy, Emilienne
Pecqueur
Assistant Unit Managers
Olivier Ricoeur, Sylvestre
Guarino
1st Assistant Director
Mylène van der Mersch
2nd Assistant Directors
Thierry Bodin, Pascal Bony
Script Supervisor
Françoise Renberg
Camera Operator
Mario Cimini
Camera Assistants
Michel Abramowicz,
Philippe Tabarly
Key Grip
Jean Hennau
Gaffers
Luciano Leomi, Eric
Gigandet
Assistant Editor
Juliette Welfling

Assistant Art Director
Claude Moesching
Set Decorator
Pierre Lefait
Costumer
Monique Dury
Make-up
Thi Loan Nguyen
Properties
René Candido, Pierre Biet
Sound
Jean-Louis Ughetto, Luc
Yersin
Assistant Sound
Philippe Donnefort
Mixer
Jacques Maumont
Sound Effects
Daniel Couteau

Cast
Christian Patey
Yvon Targe
Vincent Risterucci
Lucien
Caroline Lang
Elise Targe
Sylvie van den Elsen
the woman
Béatrice Tabourin
woman photographer
Didier Baussy
man photographer
Marc Ernest Fourneau
Norbert
Bruno Lapeyre
Martial
Michel Briguet
the woman's father

François-Marie Banier
Jeanne Aptekman
Alain Aptekman
Dominique Mullier
Jacques Behr
Gilles Durieux
Alain Bourguignon
André Cler
Claude Cler
Anne de Kervazdoue
Bernard Lamarche Vadel
Pierre Tessier
Eric Franklin
Jean-Louis Berdot
Yves Martin
Luc Solente
Valérie Mercier
Alexandre Pasche
Jean-Michel Coletti
Stéphane Villette

84 minutes
7,595 feet

Colour by
Eastmancolor
Subtitles

Credits compiled by
Markku Salmi,
BFI Filmographic Unit

Bibliography

Arnaud, Philippe, *Robert Bresson* (Paris: Cahiers du Cinéma, 1986).

Assayas, Olivier, 'The Permanence of the Devil', trans. Kent Jones, *Film Comment*, vol. 35 no. 4, July/August 1999, 48–51.

Bresson, Robert, *Notes on the Cinematographer*, trans. Jonathan Griffin (London, Melbourne, New York: Quartet Books, 1986).

Ciment, Michel, 'I Seek Not Description but Vision: Robert Bresson on *L'Argent*' trans. Pierre Hodgson, in Quandt (ed.), *Robert Bresson*.

Durgnat, Raymond, 'The Negative Vision of Robert Bresson', in Quandt (ed.), *Robert Bresson*.

Farber, Manny, *Negative Space*, expanded edn (New York: Da Capo Press, 1998).

Jameson, Fredric, 'Reading Hitchcock', *October*, no. 23, Winter 1982, 15–42.

Paini, Dominique (ed.), *Robert Bresson – Éloge* (Milan: Editions Gabriele Mazzotta; Paris: Cinématheque Française, 1997).

Pipolo, Tony, 'Rules of the Game: On Bresson's *Les Anges du péché*', in Quandt (ed.), *Robert Bresson*.

Quandt, James (ed.), *Robert Bresson* (Toronto: Cinémathèque Ontario, 1998).

Schapiro, Meyer, *On the Humanity of Abstract Painting* (New York: George Braziller, 1995).

Schrader, Paul, *Transcendental Style in Film* (New York: Da Capo Press, 1972).

Sitney, P. Adams, 'Cinematography vs. the Cinema: Bresson's Figures', in Quandt (ed.), *Robert Bresson*.

Thomson, David, *Biographical Dictionary of Film*, 3rd edn (New York: Alfred A. Knopf, 1994).

Tolstoy, Leo, *The Forged Coupon*, trans. David Patterson (New York and London: W.W. Norton, 1986).

Trilling, Lionel, *The Opposing Self* (New York and London: Harcourt Brace Jovanovich, 1979).

Also Published